RAMANA MAHARSHI

AND HIS

PHILOSOPHY OF EXISTENCE

by

T. M. P. MAHADEVAN, M.A., Ph.d.,
*Director, Centre of Advanced Study in Philosophy
University of Madras.*

Sri Ramanasramam
Tiruvannamalai
2010

First Edition	–	*1959*
Second Edition	–	*1967*
Third Edition	–	*1999 – 2000 copies*
Fourth Edition	–	*2005 – 1000 copies*
Fifth Edition	–	*2007 – 1000 copies*
Sixth Edition	–	2010 – 1000 copies

Price: Rs. 65/-

CC: 1100

ISBN: 978-81-88018-27-9

Published by
V.S. Ramanan
President
Sri Ramanasramam
Tiruvannamalai 606 603
Tamil Nadu INDIA
Telephone : 91-(0) 4175-237292 / 237200

Email: ashram@sriramanamaharshi.org
Website: www.sriramanamaharshi.org

Typeset at
Sri Ramanasramam

Printed by
Gnanodaya Press
Chennai 600 035

PUBLISHER'S NOTE

Dr. T. M. P. Mahadevan was perhaps one of the very few devotees of Sri Ramana Maharshi who had not only a clear grasp of his teachings but understood their historical relevance in the field of philosophical thought.

"Ulladu Narpardu" (Forty Verses on Reality) and its Supplement is widely considered the Maharshi's quintessential scripture, embodying the most precise expression of Reality written by a sage who experienced it. With the remarkable clarity of a refined and disciplined intellect, the author's translation and interpretation of this sublime composition will certainly inspire spiritual seekers and students of philosophy alike.

All spiritual seekers and students of philosophy will surely benefit by a careful reading of the following pages.

14 May 2007   Mahasamadhi Day

PREFACE TO THE FIRST EDITION

As a student of the Upanishads, I have often wondered at the way in which the sages should have discovered and taught the truths enshrined in them. On reading these texts one is convinced that those who were responsible for revealing them were not speaking from mere second-hand knowledge. There is an unmistakable ring of authenticity and directness about them. The Upanishadic teachings do not seem to be of the nature of idle speculations about, or wild guesses at Reality: every teacher would appear to say in effect, 'I have seen what I now declare; you are welcome to see for yourself'. It is the same ring of authenticity and directness that one finds in the teachings of the sages of modern India also, like Ramakrishna and Ramana. Ramana Maharshi, the subject of the present book, did not first read and speculate, and then experience and expound. He first experienced the ultimate Reality and then expounded it, mostly through silence and sometimes through words, spoken and written.

The Maharshi wrote very little. And much of what he wrote was in response to meet a particular demand, especially in the form of an aspirant wanting to have a doubt resolved or difficulty removed. Sri Ramana himself has explained to those devotees who were inquisitive to know the exact manner in which his writings were accomplished, especially *The Forty Verses on Existence* (*Ulladu Narpadu*) and *The Supplement* (*Anubandham*) on which I have offered comments in the pages that follow. This is what he said in one of his talks: "It was some time in 1928. Muruganar [an ardent devotee and Tamil poet] said, one day, that some stray verses composed by me now and then on various occasions should not be allowed to lapse, but should be collected together and some more added to them to bring the whole number to forty, and that the entire forty should constitute a book with an appropriate title. He accordingly gathered about thirty stray verses and requested me to compose additional verses to complete the number forty. In accordance with his wish, I wrote some more verses on different occasions, and as the mood came upon me. When the number totalled forty, Muruganar went about deleting one after another of the old collection of about thirty verses on the ground that they were not quite germane to the subject on hand or otherwise not quite suitable, and then requested me to make more verses. When this process was completed and there were forty verses as required by Muruganar, it was found that only two verses of the original collection had secured a place in the forty, and that all the rest were fresh compositions. So, the forty verses were not made according to any set scheme, nor at a stretch, nor systematically. I composed different verses on different occasions, and Muruganar and others arranged them afterwards in some order according to the thoughts expressed in them, to give a semblance of connected and systematic treatment of the subject, viz., Reality."

There was now the problem of the deleted verses; and they did not come up to forty. So, Sri Ramana had to write a few more verses. Quite a few of these were Tamil renderings from other sources such as the *Yoga Vasishta*. The supplementary forty verses came thus to be added to the forty on 'Existence'.

'Existence' in Vedanta is a term which indicates the nature of the highest Reality. *Brahman-Atman* is existence, *sat* (Sanskrit), *ulladu* (Tamil). It is not bare existence; it is existence that is consciousness (*chit*) and bliss (*ananda*). The Upanishads and the Vedanta that is based thereon and whose greatest exponent was Acharya Sankara teach about the Reality that is Existence.

Hence it is that Vedanta is called *sadvidya* (knowledge of Existence). Sri Ramana's *Forty Verses* along with *The Supplement* constitute a concise and precise statement of the truth of Vedanta. Of the present book, *The Forty Verses* and *The Supplement* form parts one and two. In part three appear some of my essays on the significance of Bhagavan Ramana's life and teaching. The original Tamil text of *The Forty Verses* and *The Supplement* is given at the end in transliterated Roman script. The short biography of Sri Ramana which I wrote for a book on *The Saints* commissioned by the Southern Languages Book Trust, Madras, has been included here as the Introduction. This has also been reprinted by Sri Ramanasramam in the form of a booklet for the convenience of the general readers.

For assistance rendered in connection with this publication, I must express my thanks to my colleagues in the University Department of Philosophy, Dr. V. A. Devasenapathi and Sri P. K. Sundaram, and to Sri T. P. Ramachandran, Research Fellow in Philosophy. I am happy that this book is being published by Sri Ramanasramam.

Madras   T. M. P. MAHADEVAN
August 24, 1959

CONTENTS

nasato vidyate bhāvo
nābhāvo vidyate satah

Of the unreal there is no existence; of the real there is no non-existence.

— *Gita*, ii, 16.

yad-viṣayā buddhir na vyabhicarati tat sat; yad-viṣayā buddhir vyabhicarati tad asat.

That is real the knowledge whereof is not inconstant, and that is unreal the knowledge whereof is inconstant.

— Sankara's *Gita-bhashya*.

INVOCATION

O! Vinayaka, who wrote on a scroll (*i.e.*, the slopes of Mt. Meru) the words of the Great Sage (*i.e.*, Vyasa) and who presides at the victorious Arunachala, do remove the disease (*i.e.*, *maya*) that is the cause of repeated births, and protect graciously the great Noble Faith (*i.e.*, the Upanishadic philosophy and religion) which brims with the honey of the Self.

This is a prayer to Lord Ganesa, the Remover of all obstacles, composed by Bhagavan Sri Ramana. Reference is made to the Puranic story that Ganesa served as a scribe to Vyasa and wrote down the *Mahabharata,* and His Grace is here invoked for the protection of the Vedanta philosophy.

SRI RAMANARPANAM

DEDICATED

TO

BHAGAVAN SRI RAMANA

WHO IS THE GROUND AND GOAL

OF

THIS ADORING ENDEAVOUR

TO

INTERPRET HIS PHILOSOPHY

INTRODUCTION

RAMANA MAHARSHI

The Scriptures tell us that it is as difficult to trace the path a sage pursues as it is to draw a line marking the course a bird takes in the air while on its wings. Most humans have to be content with a slow and laborious journey towards the goal. But a few are born as adepts in flying nonstop to the common home of all beings — the supreme Self. The generality of mankind takes heart when such a sage appears. Though it is unable to keep pace with him, it feels uplifted in his presence and has a foretaste of the felicity compared to which the pleasures of the world pale into nothing. Countless people who went to Tiruvannamalai during the lifetime of Maharshi Sri Ramana had this experience. They saw in him a sage without the least touch of worldliness, a saint of matchless purity, a witness to the eternal truth of Vedanta. It is not often that a spiritual genius of the magnitude of Sri Ramana visits this earth. But when such an event occurs, the entire humanity gets benefited and a new era of hope opens before it.

About thirty miles south of Madurai there is a village Tiruchuzhi by name with an ancient Siva temple about which two of the great Tamil saints, Sundaramurti and Manikkavachakar, have sung. In this sacred village there lived in the latter part of the nineteenth century an uncertified pleader, Sundaram Aiyar with his wife Alagammal. Piety, devotion and charity characterised this ideal couple. Sundaram Aiyar was generous even beyond his measure. Alagammal was an ideal Hindu wife. To them was born Venkataraman — who later came to be known to the world as Ramana Maharshi — on the 30th of December, 1879. It was an auspicious day for the Hindus, the *Ardra-darshanam* day. On this day every year the image of the Dancing Siva, Nataraja, is taken out of the temples in procession in order to celebrate the divine grace of the Lord that made Him appear before such saints as Gautama, Patanjali, Vyaghrapada, and Manikkavachaka. In the year 1879 on the Ardra day the Nataraja Image of the temple at Tiruchuzhi was taken out with all the attendant ceremonies, and just as it was about to re-enter, Venkataraman was born.

There was nothing markedly distinctive about Venkataraman's early years. He grew up just as an average boy. He was sent to an elementary school in Tiruchuzhi, and then for a year's education to a school in Dindigul. When he was twelve, his father died. This necessitated his going to Madurai along with the family and living with his paternal uncle Subbaiyar. There he was sent to Scott's Middle School and then to the American Mission High School. He was an indifferent student, not at all serious about his studies. But he was a healthy and strong lad. His schoolmates and other companions were afraid of his strength. If some of them had any grievance against him at any time, they would dare play pranks with him only when he was asleep. In this he was rather unusual; he would not know of anything that happened to him during sleep. He would be carried away or even beaten without his waking up in the process.

It was apparently by accident that Venkataraman heard about Arunachala when he was sixteen years of age. One day an elderly relative of his called on the family in Madurai. The boy asked him where he had come from. The relative replied 'From Arunachala'. The very name 'Arunachala' acted as a magic spell on Venkataraman, and with an evident excitement he put his next question to the elderly gentleman, 'What! From Arunachala! Where is it?' And he got the reply that Tiruvannamalai was Arunachala.

Referring to this incident the Sage says later on in one of his Hymns to Arunachala: 'Oh, great wonder! As an insentient hill it stands. Its action is difficult for anyone to understand. From my childhood it appeared to my intelligence that Arunachala was something very great. But even when I came to know through another that it was the same as Tiruvannamalai I did not understand its meaning. When, stilling my mind, it drew me up to it, and I came close, I found that it was the Immovable.'

Quickly following the incident which attracted Venkataraman's attention to Arunachala, there was another happening which also contributed to the turning of the boy's mind to the deeper values of spirituality. He chanced to lay his hands on a copy of Sekkilar's *Periyapuranam* which relates the lives of the Saiva saints. He read the book and was enthralled by it. This was the first piece of religious literature that he read. The example of the saints fascinated him; and in the inner recesses of his heart he found something responding favourably. Without any apparent earlier preparation, a longing arose in him to emulate the spirit of renunciation and devotion that constituted the essence of saintly life.

The spiritual experience that Venkataraman was now wishing devoutly to have came to him soon, and quite unexpectedly. It was about the middle of the year 1896; Venkataraman was seventeen then. One day he was sitting up alone on the first floor of his uncle's house. He was in his usual health. There was nothing wrong with it. But a sudden and unmistakable fear of death took hold of him. He felt he was going to die. Why this feeling should have come to him he did not know. The feeling of impending death, however, did not unnerve him. He calmly thought about what he should do. He said to himself, 'Now, death has come. What does it mean? What is it that is dying? This body dies.' Immediately thereafter he lay down stretching his limbs out and holding them stiff as though rigor mortis had set in. He held his breath and kept his lips tightly closed, so that to all outward appearance his body resembled a corpse. Now, what would happen? This was what he thought: 'Well, this body is now dead. It will be carried to the burning ground and there burnt and reduced to ashes. But with the death of this body am I dead? Is the body I? This body is silent and inert. But I feel the full force of my personality and even the voice of the "I" within me, apart from it. So I am the Spirit transcending the body. The body dies but the Spirit that transcends it cannot be touched by death. That means I am the deathless Spirit.' As Bhagavan Sri Ramana narrated this experience later on for the benefit of his devotees it looked as though this was a process of reasoning. But he took care to explain that this was not so. The realization came to him in a flash. He perceived the truth directly. 'I' was something very real, the only real thing. Fear of death had vanished once and for all. From then on, 'I' continued like the fundamental *sruti* note that underlies and blends with all the other notes. Thus young Venkataraman found himself on the peak of spirituality without any arduous or prolonged sadhana. The ego was lost in the flood of Self-awareness. All of a sudden the boy that used to be called Venkataraman had flowered into a sage and saint.

A complete change was noticed in the young sage's life. The things that he had valued earlier now lost their value. The spiritual values which he had ignored till then became the only objects of attention. School—studies, friends, relations — none of these had now any significance for him. He grew utterly indifferent to his surroundings. Humility, meekness, non-resistance and other virtues became his adornment. Avoiding company he preferred to sit alone, all-absorbed in concentration on the Self. He went to the Meenakshi temple every day and experienced an exaltation every time he stood before the images of the gods and the saints. Tears flowed from his eyes profusely. The new vision was constantly with him. His was the transfigured life.

Venkataraman's elder brother observed the great change that had come upon him. On several occasions he rebuked the boy for his indifferent and *yogi*-like behaviour. About six weeks after the great experience, the crisis came. It was the 29th of August, 1896. Venkataraman's English teacher had asked him, as a punishment for indifference in studies, to copy out a lesson from Bain's Grammar three times. The boy copied it out twice, but stopped there, realizing the utter futility of that task. Throwing aside the book and the papers, he sat up, closed his eyes, and turned inward in meditation. The elder brother who was watching Venkataraman's behaviour all the while went up to him and said: 'What use is all this to one who is like this?' This was obviously meant as a rebuke for Venkataraman's unworldly ways including neglect of studies. Venkataraman did not give any reply. He admitted to himself that there was no use pretending to study and be his old self. He decided to leave his home; and he remembered that there was a place to go to, *viz.* Tiruvannamalai. But if he expressed his intention to his elders, they would not let him go. So he had to use guile. He told his brother that he was going to school to attend a special class that noon. The brother thereupon asked him to take five rupees from the box below and pay it as his fee at the college where he was studying. Venkataraman went downstairs; his aunt served him a meal and gave him the five rupees. He took out an atlas which was in the house and noted that the nearest railway station to Tiruvannamalai mentioned there was Tindivanam. Actually, however, a branch line had been laid to Tiruvannamalai itself. The atlas was an old one, and so this was not marked. Calculating that three rupees would be enough for the journey, Venkataraman took that much and left the balance with a letter at a place in the house where his brother could easily find them, and made his departure for Tiruvannamalai. This was what he wrote in that letter: 'I have set out in quest of my Father in accordance with his command. This (meaning his person) has only embarked on a virtuous enterprise. Therefore, no one need grieve over this act. And no money need be spent in search of this. Your college fee has not been paid. Herewith rupees two.'

There was a curse on Venkataraman's family — in truth, it was a blessing — that one out of every generation should turn out to be a mendicant. This curse was administered by a wandering ascetic who, it is said, begged alms at the house of one of Venkataraman's forbears, and was refused. A paternal uncle of Sundaram Aiyar's became a *sannyasin*; so did Sundaram Aiyar's elder brother. Now, it was the turn of Venkataraman, although no one could have foreseen that the curse would work out in this manner. Dispassion found lodgement in Venkataraman's heart, and he became a *parivrajaka*.

It was an epic journey that Venkataraman made from Madurai to Tiruvannamalai. About noon he left his uncle's house. He walked to the railway station which was half a mile away. The train was running fortunately late that day; otherwise he would have missed it. He looked up the table of fares and came to know that the third-class fare to Tindivanam was two rupees and thirteen annas. He bought a ticket, and kept with him the balance of three annas. Had he known that there was a rail line to Tiruvannamalai itself, and had he consulted the table of fares, he would have found that the fare was exactly three rupees. When the train arrived, he boarded it quietly and took his seat. A Maulvi who was also travelling entered into conversation with Venkataraman. From him Venkataraman learnt that there was train service to Tiruvannamalai and that one need not go to Tindivanam but could change trains at Viluppuram. This was a piece of useful information. It was dusk when the train reached Tiruchirappalli. Venkataraman was hungry; he bought two country pears for half an anna; and strangely enough even with the first bite his hunger was appeased. About three o'clock in the morning the train arrived at Viluppuram. Venkataraman got off the train there with the intention of completing the rest of the journey to Tiruvannamalai by walking.

At daybreak he went into the town, and was looking out for the signpost to Tiruvannamalai. He saw a signboard reading 'Mambalappattu' but did not know then that Mambalappattu was a place *en route* to Tiruvannamalai. Before making further efforts to find out which road he was to take, he wanted to refresh himself as he was tired and hungry. He went up to a hotel and asked for food. He had to wait till noon for the food to be ready. After eating his meal, he proffered two annas in payment. The hotel proprietor asked him how much money he had. When told by Venkataraman that he had only two and a half annas, he declined to accept payment. It was from him that Venkataraman came to know that Mambalappattu was a place on the way to Tiruvannamalai. Venkataraman went back to Viluppuram station and bought a ticket to Mambalappattu for which the money he had was just enough.

It was sometime in the afternoon when Venkataraman arrived at Mambalappattu by train. From there he set out on foot for Tiruvannamalai. About ten miles he walked, and it was late in the evening. There was the temple of Arayaninallur nearby built on a large rock. He went there, waited for the doors to be opened, entered and sat down in the pillared hall. He had a vision there — a vision of brilliant light enveloping the entire place. It was no physical light. It shone for some time and then disappeared. Venkataraman continued sitting in a mood of deep meditation, till he was roused by the temple priests who were wanting to lock the doors and go to another temple three quarters of a mile away at Kilur for service. Venkataraman followed them, and while inside the temple, he got lost in *samadhi* again. After finishing their duties the priests woke him up, but would not give him any food. The temple drummer who had been watching the rude behaviour of the priests implored them to hand over his share of the temple food to the strange youth. When Venkataraman asked for some drinking water, he was directed to a Sastri's house which was at some distance. While in that house he fainted and fell down. A few minutes later, he rallied round and saw a small crowd looking at him curiously. He drank the water, ate some food, and lay down and slept.

The next morning he woke up. It was the 31st of August 1896, the *Gokulashtami* day, the day of Sri Krisna's birth. Venkataraman resumed his journey and walked for quite a while. He felt tired and hungry. So he wished for some food first, and then he would go to Tiruvannamalai, by train if that was possible. The thought occurred to him that he could dispose of the pair of gold ear rings, he was wearing and raise the money that was required. But how was this to be accomplished? He went and stood outside a house which happened to belong to one Muthukrishna Bhagavatar. He asked the Bhagavatar for food and was directed to the housewife. The good lady was pleased to receive the young *sadhu* and feed him on the auspicious day of Sri Krisna's birth. After the meal, Venkataraman went to the Bhagavatar again and told him that he wanted to pledge his ear rings for four rupees in order that he may complete his pilgrimage. The rings were worth about twenty rupees, but Venkataraman had no need for that much money. The Bhagavatar examined the ear rings, gave Venkataraman the money he had asked for, took down the youth's address, wrote out his own on a piece of paper for him, and told him that he could redeem the rings at any time. Venkataraman had his lunch at the Bhagavatar's house. The pious lady gave him a packet of sweets that she had prepared for *Gokulashtami*.

Venkataraman took leave of the couple, tore up the address the Bhagavatar had given him — for he had no intention of redeeming the ear rings — and went to the railway station. As there was no train till the next morning, he spent the night there. On the morning of the 1st. September, 1896, he boarded the train to Tiruvannamalai. The journey took only a short time. Alighting from the train, he hastened to the great temple of Arunachalesvara. All the gates stood open — even the doors of the inner shrine. The temple was then empty of all people — even the priests. Venkataraman entered the *sanctum sanctorum*, and as he stood before his Father Arunachalesvara he experienced great ecstasy and unspeakable joy. The epic journey had ended. The ship had come safely to port.

The rest of what we regard as Ramana's life — this is how we shall call him hereafter — was spent in Tiruvannamalai. Ramana was not formally initiated into *sannyasa*. As he came out of the temple and was walking along the streets of the town, someone called out and asked whether he wanted his tuft removed. He consented readily, and was conducted to the Ayyankulam tank where a barber shaved his head. Then he stood on the steps of the tank and threw away into the water his remaining money. He also discarded the packet of sweets given by the Bhagavatar's wife. The next to go was the sacred thread he was wearing. As he was returning to the temple he was just wondering why he should give his body the luxury of a bath, when there was a downpour which drenched him.

The first place of Ramana's residence in Tiruvannamalai was the great temple. For a few weeks he remained in the thousand-pillared hall. But he was troubled by urchins who pelted stones at him as he sat in meditation. He shifted himself to obscure corners, and even to an underground vault known as *Patala Lingam*. Undisturbed, he used to spend several days in deep absorption. Without moving he sat in *samadhi*, not being aware of even the bites of vermin and pests. But the mischievous boys soon discovered the retreat and indulged in their pastime of throwing potsherds at the young *Swami*. There was at the time in Tiruvannamalai a senior *Swami* by name Seshadri. Those who did not know him took him for a madman. He sometimes stood guard over the young *Swami*, and drove away the urchins. At long last he was removed from the pit by devotees without his being aware of it and deposited in the vicinity of a shrine of Subrahmanya. From then on there was someone or other to take care of Ramana. The seat of residence had to be changed frequently. Gardens, groves, shrines — these were chosen to keep the *Swami*. The *Swami* himself never spoke. Not that he took any vow of silence; he had no inclination to talk. At times the texts like *Vasishtham* and *Kaivalya-navanitam* used to be read out to him.

A little less than six months after his arrival at Tiruvannamalai, Ramana shifted his residence to a shrine called Gurumurtam at the earnest request of its keeper, a Tambiranswami. As days passed and as Ramana's fame spread, increasing numbers of pilgrims and sightseers came to visit him. After about a year's stay at Gurumurtam, the *Swami* — locally he was known as *Brahmana Swami* — moved to a neighbouring mango orchard. It was here that one of his uncles, Nelliyappa Aiyar traced him. Nelliyappa Aiyar was a second-grade pleader at Manamadurai. Having learnt from a friend that Venkataraman was then a revered Sadhu at Tiruvannamalai, he went there to see him. He tried his best to take Ramana along with him to Manamadurai. But the young sage would not respond. He did not show any sign of interest in the visitor. So, Nelliyappa Aiyar went back disappointed to Manamadurai. However, he conveyed the news to Alagammal, Ramana's mother.

The mother went to Tiruvannamalai accompanied by her eldest son. Ramana was then living at Pavalakkunru, one of the eastern spurs of Arunachala. With tears in her eyes Alagammal entreated Ramana to go back with her. But for the Sage there was no going back. Nothing moved him — not even the wailings and weepings of his mother. He kept silent giving no reply. A devotee who had been observing the struggle of the mother for several days requested Ramana to write out at least what he had to say. The Sage wrote on a piece of paper in quite an impersonal way thus:

'In accordance with the *prarabdha* of each, the One whose function it is to ordain makes each to act. What will not happen will never happen, whatever effort one may put forth. And what will happen will not fail to happen, however much one may seek to prevent it. This is certain. The path of wisdom therefore is to stay quiet.'

Disappointed and with a heavy heart, the mother went back to Manamadurai. Sometime after this event Ramana went up the hill Arunachala, and started living in a cave called Virupaksha, named after a saint who had dwelt there and who was buried there. Here also the crowds came, and among them were a few earnest seekers. These later used to put to him questions regarding spiritual experience or bring sacred books for having some points explained. Ramana sometimes wrote out his answers and explanations. One of the books that was brought to him during this period was Sankara's *Viveka-chudamani,* which later on he rendered into Tamil prose. There were also some simple unlettered folk that came to him for solace and spiritual guidance. One of them was Echammal who having lost her husband, son and daughter, was disconsolate till the Fates guided her to Ramana's presence. She made it a point to visit the *Swami* every day and took upon herself the task of bringing food for him as well as for those who lived with him.

In 1903 there came to Tiruvannamalai a great Sanskrit scholar and *savant,* Ganapati Sastri known also as Ganapati Muni because of the austerities he had been observing. He had the title *Kavya Kantha* (one who had poetry at his throat), and his disciples addressed him as *Nayana* (father). He was a specialist in the worship of the Divine as Mother. He visited Ramana in the Virupaksha cave quite a few times. Once in 1907 he was assailed by doubts regarding his own spiritual practices. He went up the hill, saw Ramana sitting alone in the cave, and expressed himself thus: 'All that has to be read I have read; even *Vedanta-sastra* I have fully understood; I have done *japa* to my heart's content; yet I have not up to this time understood what *tapas* is. Therefore I have sought refuge at your feet. Pray enlighten me as to the nature of *tapas.*' Ramana replied, now speaking, 'If one watches whence the notion "I" arises, the mind gets absorbed there; that is *tapas*. When a *mantra* is repeated, if one watches whence that mantra sound arises, the mind gets absorbed there; that is *tapas*.' To the scholar this came as a revelation; he felt the grace of the Sage enveloping him. He it was who proclaimed Ramana to be *Maharshi* and *Bhagavan*. He composed hymns in Sanskrit in praise of the Sage, and also wrote the *Ramana Gita* explaining his teachings.

Ramana's mother, Alagammal, after her return to Manamadurai, lost her eldest son. Two years later, her youngest son, Nagasundaram paid a brief visit to Tiruvannamalai. She herself went there once on her return from a pilgrimage to Varanasi, and again during a visit to Tirupati. On this occasion she fell ill and suffered for several weeks with symptoms of typhoid. Ramana showed great solicitude in nursing her and restoring her to health. He even composed a hymn in Tamil, beseeching Lord Arunachala to cure her of her disease. The first verse of the hymn runs as follows: 'Oh Medicine in the form of a Hill that arose to cure the disease of all the births that come in succession like waves! Oh Lord! It is Thy duty to save my mother who regards Thy feet alone as her refuge, by curing her fever.' He also prayed that his mother should be granted the vision divine and be weaned from worldliness. It is needless to say that both the prayers were answered. Alagammal recovered and went back to Manamadurai. But not long after, she returned to Tiruvannamalai; a little later, followed her youngest son, Nagasundaram, who had meanwhile lost his wife, leaving a son.

It was in the beginning of 1916 that the mother came and resolved to spend the rest of her life with Ramana. Soon after his mother's arrival, Ramana moved from Virupaksha to Skandasramam, a little higher up the hill. The mother received training in intense spiritual life. She donned the ochre robe, and took charge of the Ashram kitchen. Nagasundaram too became a *sannyasin*, assuming the name Niranjanananda. Among Ramana's devotees he came to be popularly known as Chinna Swami (the Younger Swami). In 1920 the mother grew weak in health and ailments incidental to old age came to her. Ramana tended her with care and affection, and spent even sleepless nights sitting up with her. The end came on May 19, 1922, which was the *Bahula-navami* day in the month of *Vaisakha*. The mother's body was taken down the hill to be interred. The spot chosen was at the southernmost point, between Palitirtham Tank and the Dakshinamurti Mantapam. While the ceremonies were being performed, Ramana himself stood silently looking on. Niranjanananda Swami took his residence near the tomb. Ramana who continued to remain at Skandasramam visited the tomb every day. After about six months he came to stay there, as he said later on, not out of his own volition but in obedience to the Divine Will. Thus was founded the Ramanasramam. A temple was raised over the tomb and was consecrated in 1949. As the years rolled by the Ashram grew steadily, and people not only from India but from every continent of the world came to see the Sage and receive help from him in their spiritual pursuits.

Ramana's first Western devotee was F. H. Humphreys. He came to India in 1911 to take up a post in the Police service at Vellore. Given to the practice of occultism, he was in search of a Mahatma. He was introduced to Ganapati Sastri by his Telugu tutor; and Sastri took him to Ramana. The Englishman was greatly impressed. Writing about his first visit to the Sage in the *International Psychic Gazette*, he said: 'On reaching the cave we sat before him, at his feet, and said nothing. We sat thus for a long time and I felt lifted out of myself. For half an hour I looked into the Maharshi's eyes, which never changed their expression of deep contemplation.... The Maharshi is a man beyond description in his expression of dignity, gentleness, self-control and calm strength of conviction.' Humphreys' ideas of spirituality changed for the better as a result of the contact with Ramana. He repeated his visits to the Sage. He recorded his impressions in his letters to a friend in England which were published in the *Gazette* mentioned above. In one of them he wrote, 'You can imagine nothing more beautiful than his smile.' And again, 'It is strange what a change it makes in one to have been in his Presence!'

It was not all good people that went to the Ashram. Sometimes bad ones turned up also — even bad *sadhus*. Twice in the year 1924 thieves broke into the Ashram in quest of loot. On the second of these occasions they even beat the Maharshi, finding that there was very little for them to take. When one of the devotees sought the sage's permission to punish the thieves, the Sage forbade him, saying: 'They have their *dharma*, we have ours. It is for us to bear and forbear. Let us not interfere with them.' When one of the thieves gave him a blow on the left thigh, he told him: 'If you are not satisfied you can strike the other leg also.' After the thieves had left, a devotee enquired about the beating. The Sage remarked, 'I also have received some *puja*', punning on the word which means 'worship' but is also used to mean 'blows'.

The spirit of harmlessness that permeated the Sage and his environs made even animals and birds make friends with him. He showed them the same consideration that he did to the humans that went to him. When he referred to any of them, he used the form 'he' or 'she' and not 'it'. Birds and squirrels built their nests around him. Cows, dogs and monkeys found asylum in the Ashram. All of them behaved intelligently — especially the cow Lakshmi. He knew their ways quite intimately. He would see to it that they were fed properly and well; and when any of them died, the body would be buried with due ceremony.

The life in the Ashram flowed on smoothly. With the passage of time more and more visitors came — some of them for a short stay and others for longer periods. The dimensions of the Ashram increased and new features and departments were added — a home for the cattle, a school for the study of the Vedas, a department for publication, and the Mother's temple with regular worship, etc. Ramana sat most of the time in the hall that had been constructed for the purpose, as the witness to all that happened around him. It was not that he was not active. He used to stitch leaf-plates, dress vegetables, read proofs received from the press, look into newspapers and books, suggest lines of reply to letters received, etc. Yet it was quite evident that he was apart from everything. There were numerous invitations for him to undertake tours. But he never moved out of Tiruvannamalai, and in the later years, not even out of the Ashram. Most of the time, everyday, people sat before him. They sat mostly in silence. Sometimes some of them asked questions; and sometimes he answered them. It was a great experience to sit before him and to look at his beaming eyes. Many did experience time coming to a stop and a stillness and peace beyond description.

The golden jubilee of Ramana's coming to stay at Tiruvannamalai was celebrated in 1946. In 1947 his health began to fail. He was not yet seventy, but looked much older. Towards the end of 1948 a small nodule appeared below the elbow of his left arm. As it grew in size, the doctor in charge of the Ashram dispensary cut it out. But in a month's time it reappeared. Surgeons from Madras were called, and they operated. The wound did not heal, and the tumour came again. On further examination it was diagnosed that the affection was a case of sarcoma. The doctors suggested amputating the arm above the affected part. Ramana replied with a smile: 'There is no need for alarm. The body is itself a disease. Let it have its natural end. Why mutilate it? Simple dressing of the affected part will do.' Two more operations had to be performed, but the tumour appeared again. Indigenous systems of medicine were tried; and homeopathy too. The disease did not yield itself to treatment. The Sage was quite unconcerned, and was supremely indifferent to suffering. He sat as a spectator watching the disease waste the body. But his eyes shone as bright as ever; and his grace flowed towards all beings. Crowds came in large numbers. Ramana insisted that they should be allowed to have his *darshan*. Devotees profoundly wished that the Sage should cure his body through an exercise of supernormal powers. Some of them imagined that they themselves had had the benefit of those powers which they attributed to Ramana. Ramana had compassion for those who grieved over the suffering and he sought to comfort them by reminding them of the truth that Bhagavan was not the body: 'They take this body for Bhagavan and attribute suffering to him. What a pity! They are despondent that Bhagavan is going to leave them and go away — where can he go, and how?'

The end came on the 14th of April, 1950. That evening the Sage gave *darshan* to the devotees that came. All that were present in the Ashram knew that the end was nearing. They sat singing Ramana's hymn to Arunachala with the refrain *Arunachala Siva*. The Sage asked his attendants to make him sit up. He opened his luminous and gracious eyes for a brief while; there was a smile; a tear of bliss trickled down from the outer corner of his eyes; and at 8-47 the breathing stopped. There was no struggle, no spasm, none of the signs of death. At that very moment, a comet moved slowly across the sky, reached the summit of the holy hill, Arunachala, and disappeared behind it.

Ramana Maharshi seldom wrote; and what little he did write in prose or verse was written to meet the specific demands of his devotees. He himself declared once: 'Somehow, it never occurs to me to write a book or compose poems. All the poems I have made were on the request of someone or other in connection with some particular event.' The most important of his works is *The Forty Verses on Existence*. In the *Upadesasaram*, which is also a poem, the quintessence of Vedanta is set forth. The sage composed five hymns to Arunachala. Some of the works of Sankara like *Vivekachudamani* and *Atma Bodha* were rendered into Tamil by him. Most of what he wrote is in Tamil. But he wrote also in Sanskrit, Telugu, and Malayalam.

The philosophy of Sri Ramana, which is the same as that of Advaita-Vedanta, has for its aim Self-realization. The central path taught in this philosophy is the enquiry into the nature of Self, the content of the notion 'I'. Ordinarily the sphere of the 'I' varies and covers a multiplicity of factors. But these factors are not really the 'I'. For instance, we speak of the physical body as 'I'; we say, 'I am fat', 'I am lean', etc. It will not take long to discover that this is a wrong usage. The body itself cannot say 'I', for it is inert. Even the most ignorant man understands the implication of the expression 'my body'. It is not easy, however, to resolve the mistaken identity of the 'I' with egoity (*ahankara*). That is because the inquiring mind is the ego, and in order to remove the wrong identification it has to pass a sentence of death, as it were, on itself. This is by no means a simple thing. The offering of the ego in the fire of wisdom is the greatest form of sacrifice.

The discrimination of the Self from the ego, we said, is not easy. But it is not impossible. All of us can have this discrimination if we ponder over the implication of our sleep experience. In sleep we are, though the ego has made its exit. The ego does not function there. Still there is the 'I' that witnesses the absence of the ego as well as of the objects. If the 'I' were not there, one would not recall on waking from one's sleep experience, and say: 'I slept happily; I did not know anything.' We have, then, two 'I's: the pseudo-'I' which is the ego and the true 'I' which is the Self. The identification of the 'I' with the ego is so strong that we seldom see the ego without its mask. Moreover, all our relative experience turns on the pivot of the ego. With the rise of the ego on waking from sleep, the entire world rises with it. The ego, therefore, looks so important and unassailable.

But this is really a fortress made of cards. Once the process of enquiry starts, it will be found to crumble and dissolve. For undertaking this enquiry, one must possess a sharp mind — much sharper than the one required for unravelling the mysteries of matter. It is with the one-pointed intellect that the truth is to be seen (*drisyate tu agraya buddhya*). It is true that even the intellect will have to get resolved before the final wisdom dawns. But up to that point it has to inquire — and inquire relentlessly. Wisdom, surely, is not for the indolent!

The enquiry 'Who am I?' is not to be regarded as a mental effort to understand the mind's nature. Its main purpose is 'to focus the entire mind at its source'. The source of the pseudo-'I' is the Self. What one does in Self-enquiry is to run against the mental current instead of running along with it, and finally transcend the sphere of mental modifications. When the pseudo-'I' is tracked down to its source, it vanishes. Then the Self shines in all its splendour, which shining is called realization and release.

The cessation or non-cessation of the body has nothing to do with release. The body may continue to exist and the world may continue to appear, as in the case of the Maharshi. That makes no difference at all to the Self that has been realized. In truth, there is neither the body nor the world for him; there is only the Self, the eternal Existence (*sat*), the Intelligence (*chit*), the unexcellable bliss (*ananda*). Such an experience is not entirely foreign to us. We have it in sleep, where we are conscious neither of the external world of things nor of the inner world of dreams. But that experience lies under the cover of ignorance. So it is that we come back to the fantasies of dream and of the world of waking. Non-return to duality is possible only when nescience has been removed. To make this possible is the aim of Vedanta. To inspire even the lowliest of us with hope and help us out of the slough of despondency, is the supreme significance of such illustrious exemplars as the Maharshi.

PART I

FORTY VERSES ON EXISTENCE

(*Ulladu Narpadu*)

INTRODUCTION

Ulladu Narpadu is a poem of forty verses on the nature of existence. The Tamil *ulladu*, like the Sanskrit *sat*, means what exists or existence and reality. Existence and reality are the same in Vedanta. As the *Bhagavad Gita* puts it, 'Of the unreal there is no existence; of the real there is no non-existence'[1]. It is true that we predicate existence of the particulars that constitute the world. We say: 'The body exists', 'The house exists', etc. But from the metaphysical point of view, existence is the reality, and is the true subject in all judgements. The objective idealists in the West, like Bradley and Bosanquet, would say that reality is the subject in all judgements. A judgement such as 'Man is rational' may be recast to read thus: 'Reality is such that man is rational'. According to these idealists, existence is not reality, but is a form of the appearance of the real[2]. Or, at best, it is a species of the real[3]. The Vedanta, however, holds that existence is neither an appearance of the real nor a species thereof, but that it is the same as reality. In our empirical judgements we wrongly push existence to the predicative side. The truth is that *existence* alone is real, the body, the house, etc., being appearances thereof[4].

---

[1] ii. 16. *nasato vidyate bhavo nabhavo vidyate satah.*
[2] See F. H. Bradley, *Appearance and Reality*, p. 400.
[3] See McTaggart, *The Nature of Existence*, Vol. 1, Ch. i.
[4] See the present writer's *The Philosophy of Advaita*, (Ganesh & Co., Madras, 2nd Ed. 1957), Ch. III, esp. pp. 114-115.

In the *Chandogya Upanishad*, the section which teaches the doctrine of identity 'That thou art' begins with the text: 'Existence alone, dear one, was this in the beginning, one only without a second'[1]. Commenting on this text, *Panchadasi*, a metrical work on Advaita, makes out that the reference to past tense in the words 'was' 'in the beginning' is for the sake of instruction, and that the repetitive language 'Existence was' is also for the same purpose. The purport of the passage is: 'Existence which is the essential nature of reality has neither external relations nor internal differentiations. It is unrelated to anything, for there is nothing else with which it can be related. The real which is the most perfect Being cannot be delimited by determinations and relations. To limit it is to finitize it. It has nothing of a like kind or of a different kind, and it has no internal variety.'[2] When the Vedanta speaks of existence as reality, it does not mean brute existence; it is existence that is intelligence and bliss. It is this existence-intelligence-bliss (*Sat-chit-ananda*) that is the non-dual Absolute, one only without a second. All distinctions such as 'I' and 'thou' are but appearances. The Self alone is. The non-duality of the Absolute, the non-reality of the world, and the non-difference of the so-called individual soul from the absolute reality — these constitute the truth of Advaita.

Sri Ramana's *Ulladu Narpadu* is an authentic exposition of the Advaita experience. We do not agree with the view which seeks to distinguish Sri Ramana's teaching from Sankara's Advaita.[3] Nor do we deem it proper to say that while for Sri Ramana all views are the same, his teaching contained in the

---

[1] VI, ii, 1.

[2] See *The Philosophy of Advaita*, p. 118.

[3] See Kapali Sastri's Commentary on *Sad-darshanam* (Sri Ramanasramam, 1931), p. 17.

Ulladu Narpadu is meant only for the followers of Advaita[1]. We believe that Advaita is not a sectarian doctrine. It is the culmination of all doctrines, the crown of all views. Though other views may imagine themselves to be opposed to Advaita, Advaita is opposed to none. Advaita is not an *ism*. When we translate *Advaita* as *non-dualism*, the negation signified by the prefix *non* applies not only to duality but also to *ism*[2]. As Gaudapada, pre-Sankara teacher of Advaita, says, Advaita has no quarrel with any system of philosophy. While the pluralistic worldviews may be in conflict with one another, Advaita is not opposed to any of them. It recognises the measure of truth that there is in each of them; but only, that truth is not the whole. Hostility arises out of partial vision. When the whole truth is realized, there can be no hostility[3]. This is exactly the teaching of Sri Ramana, as will be seen in the sequel. Through the medium of these forty verses, the Sage of Arunachala transmits to us the plenary experience which is that of Advaita.

INVOCATION

1. Is there an existent awareness other than existence? Because the existence-reality exists in the Heart free from thoughts, the existence-reality is called the Heart. How to contemplate it? To exist as it exists in the heart is to contemplate it. Thus should you know.

It is usual to begin a work with an invocation, in order that the work may be completed successfully and to be in conformity with pious practice. This and the next verse are not

---

[1] See the Tamil Commentary, by 'WHO' (1950, p. 3.)
[2] See the present writer's paper 'Western Vedanta' in *Vedanta for Modern Man* (Harper & Brothers, N.Y.), p. 17.
[3] See *Mandukya-karika*, III, 17 and 18; IV, 5.

counted among the forty verses on Existence. They are invocatory
verses. The invocation need not necessarily be in the form of a
prayer addressed to a personal God. It may also be in the mode
of remembrance of the nature of the impersonal Absolute.
According to Advaita-Vedanta, in the ultimate experience, even
the conception of a God is transcended. That does not mean,
however, that there is no place for God in Advaita. Sankara, the
great exponent of the non-dualism of Spirit, which is Advaita,
has left behind him soul-moving poems of adoration to the
myriad forms of the personal Deity, poems that constitute a
grand testimony to the intense devotion of their author. The
worshipper-worshipped relation is a genuine relation; and it is a
sublimation of all other relations. But even this, says Advaita, is
transcended in the final distinctionless experience. What is more
cannot be less. If Advaita is more than theism, it cannot be
atheism or anti-theism[1].

The fact that in the first verse of the Invocation Sri Ramana
teaches the nature of the impersonal Absolute, and in the second
verse the nature of the personal God shows at once the place of
theism in Advaita and Sri Ramana's testimony to the Advaita
experience. In the first verse reality is identified as existence-
awareness; it is described as the Heart; and the true
contemplation of it is stated to be the realization of one's identity
with it. In the second verse, reference is made to Maheswara,
the great Lord, who is the ruler even of Death, and who is sought
as refuge by those who are afraid of death; and the way to
deathlessness is also indicated.

Now, let us study the first verse of the Invocation. The first
proposition is put in the form of a rhetorical question whose

---

[1] See '*Western Vedanta*', op. cit., p. 17.

meaning is: Other than existence there is no existent awareness. As we have already said in the Introduction, in empirical judgements we wrongly predicate existence of the objects of experience, whereas in truth these latter are but the appearance of existence. Defining reality as that which is constant and abiding in things that change, the Vedanta discovers that existence is reality. *Sat* and *satya*, existence and truth, which are synonyms, mean that which transcends the three parts of time, past, present and future. While particular modes of existence are perishing presentations, existence as such is imperishable and absolute.

Reality is not mere existence; it is also intelligence or awareness. To consider reality to be simple objective being would result in scepticism and agnosticism. All forms of materialism and naturalism flounder and fail because even to state them is required an intelligence which cannot be reduced to a datum of sense. Nor is it true to identify reality with a stream of ideas; for that would lead to subjectivism and solipsism. Reality is neither inert existence nor a subjective series of presentations. It is *sat-chit*, existence-consciousness. Even reality is not an existent but existence, so also it is not consciousness-*of* but consciousness-*as*. In other words, the 'Real' is pure existence and pure consciousness.

Sri Ramana designates the Real as the heart, because its seat is the heart. The location of the heart in the physical body is the chest, two digits to the right from the median. A person, when asked for his identity, instinctively points by gesture of hand to the right side of his chest. The sage, when he is with bodily awareness, localizes the absolute experience within the heart. In truth, however, the location of the Self in the heart is only from the standpoint of body-consciousness. The Self is the heart in the sense that it is the core of one's being, the centre of all-that-is. Even when it is said to be seated in the heart, it is not the heart which is of the stuff of relative experience that is meant, but the heart which is emptied of all empiric contents, the heart that is pure and free from thoughts[1].

How is one to contemplate the heart centre? It is not an 'other' which can be contemplated by way of ideation. Empirical knowledge which involves the distinction of subject and object is not applicable to the distinctionless Absolute. One has to know it by being it, or in other words, by realizing one's identity with it.

2. *Those people, who have intense fear of death seek as their refuge only the feet of the great Lord, who is without death and birth. Those who are dead to themselves, along with their adjuncts, will they harbour thought of death? They are deathless!*

Here, reference may be seen to two levels of experience, the theistic and the absolutistic. At the theistic level, the fear of death drives one to the feet of God. At the absolutistic level, no such fear arises, because the plenary experience is the state of fearlessness (*abhaya*) and deathlessness (*amrityupada*).

The great turning point in the life of Sri Ramana was itself made possible by the fear of death. One day when he was seventeen and quite healthy, the fear of death seized him, and he took up the challenge. He dramatized death and worked out the consequences in his own mind. And, the great discovery dawned upon him that the Self is untouched by death, and that he is the deathless Self. Recalling this experience long afterwards for the benefit of spiritual aspirants, Sri Ramana says: 'The "I" or my "self" was holding the focus of attention by a powerful

---

[1] See *Maharshi's Gospel* (Book II, 1944), pp. 43-62.

fascination from that time onwards. Fear of death had vanished at once and forever. Absorption in the Self has continued from that moment right up to this time. Other thoughts may come and go like the various notes of a piece of music, but the "I" continues like the *sruti* or the unvarying, basic or fundamental note, which accompanies and blends with all other notes.'[1]

One sees the face of death everywhere, and yet one does not want to die. The desire for deathlessness is universal. Then, there must be something wrong with the common sense view of death. Meditation on death is an essential part of the discipline for the philosopher and the saint. The *Bhagavad Gita* includes the realization of the misery and defect of death among the ingredients of wisdom (*jnana*)[2]. To the question 'Is philosophy the practice of death?' Plato answers 'yes', and adds that the philosopher is he who knows how to die with ease. Before proceeding to the land of Death in order to make true the angry and unthinking words of his father, Nachiketas consoles his sire saying: 'Like corn does a mortal ripen; like corn does he spring to life again.'[3] If one understands the truth about death, one would be freed from the fear of death. This, however, comes only on the realization of the oneness of Self. In order to pave the way for that experience, the Scriptures urge man to seek refuge in God, so that death for him will lose its terror.

God, by common consent, is without birth and death. Even those faiths which believe in a changing God place Him beyond time. God is indestructible, and has no fear of death. One of the stories about Siva is that He drank the poison emitted by the serpent Vasuki when it was used as the rope in the process of

---

[1] See *Self-Realization*, p. 20.
[2] iii. 8.
[3] *Katha*, I, 6.

the churning of the milk-ocean[1]. Alluding to this episode, a Hymn to Siva, attributed to Sankara, says: 'Is not this one great help enough, O Lord of souls? Seeing the assemblage of moving and non-moving beings resident in your stomach and resident without, in order to protect them, you placed in your throat the greatly flaming and fearful poison, as a remedy for preventing all the immortals from taking to their heels! You neither swallowed it nor spat it out.'[2] In order to obtain ambrosia, the gods and the demons churned the milk-ocean with Mount Mandara as the churning rod and Vasuki as the rope. From the fangs of Vasuki came out the world-destroying poison. To escape from its deadly effect, all began to flee, including the gods. Lord Siva, then, gathered the poison in his palm and drank it. But He did not swallow it, in order that the beings located within His body may not perish; He retained the poison in His throat, thus receiving the epithets, Sri-kantha, Nila-kantha, Nila-griva (He with the auspicious or blue throat).

The universal conception of God is that He protects those who seek Him as their refuge. He is described as the Friend-in-need (*apat-bandhava*), Helper of the helpless (*anatha-rakshaka*), and so on. During the Blitz in England a hymn was composed and set to music. It began with the lines:

God is our refuge, be not afraid,
He will be with you all through the raid[3].

Some pious people seem to welcome crises so that they may turn to God and seek His protection. At the end of the Mahabharata War, when Sri Krishna asked Kunti (mother of

[1] See *Ramayana*, I, 45.
[2] *Sivanandalahari*, 31.
[3] Mass-Observation, *Puzzled People* (Victor Gollanz Ltd., London, 1948), p. 59.

the Pandavas) to ask for a boon, she said 'Let misfortunes befall us ever'. An English woman of fifty-five, when asked if she ever prayed, said, 'Well, I do when I think I've got more trouble than I can handle. But it's got to be something very bad to make me pray'.[1] What can be worse than the fear of death? And, to whom else can people go for refuge than to the One who is eternally free from death? The story is told in the *Puranas* of Markandeya who, according to the decree of Destiny, was to die at the age of sixteen. He took refuge in Lord Siva, and was saved from the clutches of death. He became immortal, an eternal youth of sixteen.

The fear of death comes to one only at the empirical level of plurality. Scripture declares: 'Verily, fear arises only from a second[2]'; When, indeed, he makes but the smallest distinction in it (the Self), there is fear for him'[3]; 'He who sees difference, as it were, here, goes from death to death'[4]. Fear (*bhaya*), plurality (*bheda*), and ignorance (*avidya*) constitute a triad making for bondage. Fearlessness (*abhaya*) arises when the non-dual Self (*advaya atman*) is realized through knowledge (*jnana*). The perception of an 'other', however attractive or friendly that 'other' may be for the time being, is the cause of fear. It is the sense of 'otherness' that is responsible for insecurity and all that goes with it. And, otherness or difference is brought about by ignorance. The so-called individual wrongly imagines that he is a denizen of a pluralistic universe, identifies himself with a particular psycho-physical organism, and is expectant of danger from every quarter including Time otherwise called Death.

---

[1] Mass-Observation, *op. cit.*, p. 57.
[2] *Brh.*, I, iv. 2.
[3] *Tait.*, II, 7.
[4] *Katha*, iv, 10; *Brh.*, IV, iv, 19.

Physical death is not so terrible as it appears, and solves no problem. It is but a change like that from childhood to youth. The Self's identification with the ego and its adjuncts which together constitute the carrier of the soul from one physical body to another — which identification is, in fact, nescience or ignorance — is the root of all evil. It is the termination of this identification that constitutes *moksha* (liberation). This dying is truly auspicious. It is dying to live. When the ego dies, there is no more transmigration, no more sorrow. To the question 'When shall I be free?' Sri Ramakrisna answered, 'When "I" shall cease to be.' To him who has attained freedom from the ego, there is no death: for he has realized that the real is the non-dual Spirit which suffers no change and is beyond the snares of Time.

THE TEXT

1. Because we perceive the world, the acceptance of a multi-powered First Principle is settled. The picture of name and form, the observer, the basic canvas and the revealing light — all these are He Himself.

This is the first of the forty verses. Its theme is the ground of the universe and the nature of that ground. One of the perpetual questions raised by philosophers and religionists is about the origin of the universe.

The *Svetasvatara Upanishad* begins by posing this question, and, after setting forth alternative views, gives its own conclusive answer: What is the cause? Is it *Brahman*? Whence are we born? Whereby do we live? And on what are we established? Overruled by whom, in pleasures and pains, do we live our various conditions, O ye knowers of Brahman? Time, or nature, or necessity, or chance, or the elements, or a womb, or a person are to be regarded (as the cause); not a conjunction of these, because of the existence of the soul. Even the soul is impotent over the cause of pleasure and pain. Those who pursued the path of meditation saw the self-power of God concealed in his own qualities. He is the one who rules over all these causes, from "time" to the "soul".[1] The manifold universe cannot be the product either of an inert substance or of a limited sentient being. It requires as its basis and origin an omniscient, omnipotent Being. That is what we call God.

The second aphorism of the *Vedanta-sutra* deals with the same topic. It defines Brahman as that whence the origin, etc., of the universe take place. Explaining the meaning of this aphorism, Acharya Sankara says: Of this world which is differentiated by names and forms, which contains many agents and enjoyers, is the abode of fruits of actions regulated in accordance with place, time and cause, and the nature of whose structure cannot be even imagined by the mind, the origin, subsistence, and dissolution proceed from that omniscient, omnipotent cause, which is Brahman[2]. Here, again, the meaning is that if we have to postulate a First Cause, it must be an omniscient, omnipotent Being.

Meykandar's *Sivajnanabodham* which is the basic text of the Saiva-siddhanta sets forth at the outset the causal argument for the reality of God. The first *sutra* reads thus: As the universe which is spoken of as 'he', 'she' and 'it' is subject to the three modifications (origin, growth and dissolution), it must be what is created. Owing to its conjunction with the impurity of *anava* (ignorance), it comes out of Hara (i.e., Siva) to whom it returns at the end. Hence, the wise say that Hara is the First Cause.

Western philosophers and theologians also have argued that God must be postulated as the ground of the universe.

---

[1] *Svet.*, I, 1-3.
[2] Sankara's Commentary on *Ved. Su.*, I, i, 2.

One of the proofs for the existence of God given by Descartes runs as follows: 'I have in me the idea of God. Now, nothing can come from nothing; whatever exists must have a cause for existing. And, the cause must be at least as great as the effect. I myself cannot be the cause of the idea of God; for I am a finite, imperfect being, while the idea of God is that of a perfect, infinite being. Hence this idea must have been placed in my mind by an infinite being or God, and God must exist. Reflecting upon the idea of God, we also realize that he must be eternal, omniscient, omnipotent, and the source of all goodness and truth; the creator of all things.'[1]

Sri Ramana refers to this well-known argument when he says, 'Because we perceive the world, the acceptance of multi-powered First Principle is settled.' The Sage does not mean to teach, however, that the argument is without flaw or that it must be accepted as expressing the final truth. The notion of causality is riddled with contradictions. Even the expression 'First Cause' is a contradiction in terms. And yet, there is an innate tendency of the mind to search for causes. So long as we are conditioned by relative existence, we cannot help seeking explanations of things in terms of their causes; and, however unsatisfactory and untenable this procedure may be in the last resort, we have to postulate a First cause. While the naturalists trace the origin of all phenomena to Nature or *prakriti*, the theists consider God to be the author of the universe. The advantage of theism over naturalism is that it attempts to explain the lower in terms of the higher — the space-time world in terms of life, life in terms of mind, and all in terms of the Deity. As Browning puts it,

---

[1] See Frank Thilly, *A History of Philosophy* (Henry Holt & Co., New York, 1931), pp. 177-8.

All tended to mankind,
And man produced, all has its end thus far:
But in completed man begins anew
A tendency to God.

There are two types of theism: one which holds that God
is external to the world, and is only its instrumental cause, and
the other, according to which, God is the material as well as the
instrumental cause. The Nyaya-Vaisheshika theism may be cited
as a representative of the first type. It is admitted in this system
that God is the ultimate cause of the creation, sustentation and
destruction of the world. But he makes the world, not out of
nothing, nor out of himself, but out of primal atoms, space,
time, ether, minds and souls which are co-eternal with him.
One of the analogies given is that of the making of pots by a
potter. The world which is a product and consists of component
parts must have had a maker. That maker of the world must be
an intelligent being, 'possessed of that combination of volition,
desire to act, and knowledge of the proper means which sets in
motion all other causes, but is itself set in motion by none.'[1] In
short, God is the unmoved mover of the universe.

The Sakta, Visishtadvaita and Advaita-Vedanta teach that
God is both the material and the efficient cause of the world,
for, to regard him as the efficient cause alone would be to set a
limit to him. Iswara is *abhinna-nimitta-upadana karana*. If God
is the cause of the world, he must be its sole cause, God is self-
established and self-complete. He is not in need of any extraneous
matter to shape the universe. The *Chandogya* says: 'In the
beginning, this world was just Being (*sat*), one only without a

---

[1] See S. Radhakrishnan, *Indian Philosophy* (George Allen and Unwin, 2nd
Ed., 1931), Vol. II, p. 168.

second. It thought unto itself: "Would that I were many! Let me procreate myself!" From It emanated heat, water, food and all beings.'[1] So, the primal Being is one; and out of that the world of plurality has come into existence. The spider weaving its web out of its own vitals, the growth of vegetation on the earth and of hairs on a living body are given as examples, in the *Mundaka*, for showing that Brahman unfolds the universe out of its own substance: Just as a spider puts forth and withdraws (its thread), just as herbs arise on the earth, just as on a living person the hairs of the head and body (grow), so from the Imperishable arises everything here[2].

The difficulty of a theism such as the one set forth above, and of all monism, is the problem how the One became the Many. In order to get over this difficulty a plurality of powers is ascribed to the One Reality. The One appears as many through its manifold powers. A *mantra* of the *Rig-veda*, which is repeated in the *Brihadaranyaka*, says: 'The Lord, on account of his *mayas* (plural), is seen as manifold.'[3] In the *Svetasvatara*, the one supreme God who is Rudra is said to rule over all the worlds with his ruling powers (*isanibhih*: plu.). After creating all beings, it is declared, he merges them together at the end of time.[4] In the *Sakta-tantra*, as in many other systems of philosophy, *Sakti* is the power which is responsible for the manifestation of the world. The ultimate reality which is *Siva-Sakti* or *Chit-Sakti* is non-dual, absolute consciousness. It has two aspects *Siva* or *Chit* is stasis; *Sakti* is kinesis. Or, to put it differently, when Siva is kinetic, he is called Sakti. The real as static is known as *prakasa*, just illumination, and as kinetic, *vimarsa*,

[1] *Chand.*, VI, i-iii.
[2] *Mund.*, I,i,7.
[3] RV., VI, 48, 18; *Brh.*, II, v. 19.
[4] *Svet.*, iii, 1-2.

manifestation. The latter which is also named *Maya-sakti* is that which unfolds, sustains and withdraws the universe.

The *Yogini-hridaya-tantra,* says: *desa-kala-padarthatma yad-yad-vastu yatha yatha tat-tadrupena ya bhatitam sraye samyidam kalam* 'The form of various objects, as space, time and things.' The *yidam kalam.* 'I seek refuge in that *Chit-sakti* who shines in the form of various objects, as space, time and things'. The *Maya-sakti* is composed of the three *gunas, sattva, rajas* and *tamas,* as is the Prakriti of the Sankhyas. This is *kamakala* which is *trigunatmaka-vibhuti,* splendour of the ultimate reality in the form of the three *gunas.* It expresses itself in the forces of desire (*iccha*), will (*kriya*) and knowledge (*jnana*). And, through these forces, the entire world of plurality is created, sustained and destroyed. Thus, the One becomes the Many by its *Sakti* which is the seed of plurality. Hence, Sri Ramana refers to the root-reality as the *multi-powered First Principle.*

Because of the design and purpose one sees in the world-manifestation, creation is sometimes compared to art production. But there is an essential difference. In the case of artwork, as for instance painting, there are many distinct causes — the *material,* the canvas, paint, etc., the *formal,* the configuration, etc., the *efficient,* the artist, brush, etc.; and the *final,* the honouring of someone, earning of livelihood, etc. But in the case of the world-manifestation, there are no distinct causes, the ground being non-dual. 'He painted the world-picture on himself', says the *Yoginihridaya,* 'with the brush which is his will and was pleased therewith.'[1] In the sixth chapter of the *Panchadasi* entitled *Chitradipa* the analogy of painting is skilfully employed to explain the successive stages in cosmic manifestation. The one non-dual Self becomes successively Isvara, Hiranyagarbha and

---

[1] See Sir John Woodroffe, *Sakti and Sakta,* 3rd Ed., Ganesh ,& Co., Madras, 1959, p. 41.

Virat in relation to the three stages in the evolution of the universe, *viz.*, the causal, subtle and the gross. And, this is compared to (1) the bleaching of the canvas and stiffening it with starch, (2) sketching the outlines of the figures on the canvas and (3) filling the picture with paint. Iswara is Brahman or Atman as qualified by *maya*. He is the material-*cum*-efficient cause of the world. Just as the bleached canvas, stiffened with starch, serves as the basis and background of a painting, so is Iswara the substratum of world-creation. Then, the outlines of the universe-to-be appear in him; and he is called the Golden Womb, Hiranyagarbha. He comprises all the Jivas with their subtle bodies and the subtle elements. This is like the sketch on the canvas. And finally, the form of Virat emerges which is the full-blown stage of the universe, and is comparable to the completed picture[1]. Only, we must remember that as regards the cosmic art, the artist and the canvas, the sketch and the paint, the patron and the critic are all one and the same reality. As Sri Ramana says in the present verse: *The picture of name and form, the observer, the basic canvas, and the revealing light — all these are He Himself.*

Philosophers have analysed the world in various ways and the list of categories differs from system to system. To cite only a few; the Sankhyas recognise two categories: *purusha* and *prakriti*; the Jainas also two, but those are called *jiva* and *ajiva*; according to the Vaisheshikas, the categories are seven, *dravya, guna, karma, samanya, vishesha, samavaya* and *abhava*; the Naiyayikas gave a much longer list of sixteen categories, but these categories are epistemological topics rather than ontological kinds of reality. In the Vedanta all phenomena are reduced to three or two categories. Name (*nama*), form (*rupa*), and activity

---

[1] See the present writer's *The Philosophy of Advaita*, p. 206.

(*karma*) constitute the stuff of the universe. Or, leaving out even activity which is a derivative category we may say that names and forms constitute the world[1]. Form (*rupa*) stands for all physical phenomena, and name (*nama*) for all mental phenomena. Other than these, there is nothing in the world. Hence, Sri Ramana describes the world as *the picture of name and form.*

> 2. *All systems of thought postulate the three principles (i.e., the world, soul, and God). Only one principle appears as three principles. To say that the three principles ever remain as three principles is but so long as the egoity lasts. After the destruction of egoity, to remain in one's own state is best.*

In the first of the forty verses Sri Ramana has taught us that the manifold universe has as its ground a multi-powered First Principle, and that the One Principle manifests itself as the name-and-form-world. By *name* we mean all psychical phenomena, and by *form* all physical facts. If we equate the First Principle with God, psychical entities with souls, and the collocation of physical facts with the material world, then we have the three well-known categories recognised, either explicitly or implicitly, in all the systems of thought. Sri Ramana refers to this in the present verse, and shows that from a higher standpoint these three principles or categories dissolve themselves into the non-dual reality.

All systems of thought postulate the three principles, viz., God, souls, and the world. By 'systems of thought' we should understand here both philosophical schools and religions. That most of the systems accept the three principles is quite evident. They are the *tattva-traya,* triple realities, spoken of variously as *Iswara* (God), *chit* (conscious beings), and *achit* (non-conscious

---

[1] *The Pholosophy of Advaita,* p. 235.

matter)[1], *pati* (lord), *pasu* (souls) and *pasa* (bonds)[2], and so on. In the systems of Western thought, the three realities are designated God, Man and Nature. This is how the Father of Modern European philosophy, Descartes, seeks to establish the three realities; he starts his philosophical enquiry doubting the existence of everything, but finds that the existence of the doubter cannot be doubted. I think, therefore, I am. From this self-evident truth Descartes establishes the existence of God and the world. One of the proofs for the existence of God we have already given. From our idea of a perfect Being, his actual existence is inferred. The existence of external bodies is also postulated on the ground of our sensations of them. God cannot be the cause of these sensations, for we are not aware that he is their cause. If he were the cause, he would be a deceiver. And, God is not a deceiver. So, our sensations must be caused by external bodies which are real. The Cartesian teaching is typical of all pluralistic systems. They may not give reasons, as Descartes attempted to give; or the reasons they give may not be adequate. But all of them believe that there are three realities, God, souls, and the world. The monistic systems too admit of these three principles one of which (*viz.*, God or Spirit) is regarded as the whole, the other two being its parts or expressions. For instance, in the system of Hegel, it is the logical idea that first reveals itself in its otherness, *viz.*, nature, and then returns into itself and becomes mind or spirit. For Ramanuja, Brahman is the whole (*amsi*) of which the souls and the world are parts (*amsa*).

There are some systems which do not overtly accept a God. The Sankhya, for example, believes only in two ultimates, *prakriti* (primal nature) and *purusha* (soul). In the presence of *purusha,*

[1] In the Visishtadvaita.
[2] In the Saiva-siddhanta.

prakriti is said to evolve into the variegated universe without requiring a God as the prime mover or as the primary ground. Buddhism, to take another instance, now from the so-called heterodox tradition, is supposed to be a godless religion. But, it is interesting to note that into both these systems, God was eventually introduced. In the Patanjala Yoga, which is the complement of the Sankhya, the need for God is felt, and his existence is sought to be proved on the principle that every set of grades must have an upper limit as well as a lower limit, that there are more and less in knowledge, and that there must be an upper limit to knowledge which is omniscience, the characteristic feature of God. God, in the Yoga system, is perfect being (*prakrista-sattva*) the guide of the evolution of *prakriti*, and an object of meditation for those who practise yoga. In the Sankhya tradition itself, the later writers such as Vijnana-bhiksu admit the necessity for God openly, and explain Kapila's denial of Iswara as but a device to turn away the minds of man from an excessive devotion to God which is supposed to be an impediment to the rise of discriminative wisdom. The Buddha was silent on the question of God, as on many other metaphysical problems. This was interpreted in some quarters as a denial of God. But later Buddhism deified the Buddha and introduced even the concept of Trinity, besides innumerable gods and godlings. Thus all systems accept, either overtly or covertly, the three principles, God, soul, and the world.

'What about the Charvaka', it may be asked, 'which is a materialistic system; and the Advaita Vedanta in which there is no place for God?' Our reply is this: (1) The Charvaka is hardly a *system*. It is a passing mood that comes upon the mind of man in its career of reflection on the nature of reality. The mind cannot rest there; it must move on. The Charvaka is irrefutable, not because it is a sound philosophy, but because it cannot even be consistently stated. As for Advaita, we have already said that it is not an *ism* or system in the sense of a closed school of philosophy[1], and that it is more than theism and not less[2]. It is because Advaita is not a philosophical system (though conventionally it is often referred to as such) that it sees a measure of truth in every philosophical attitude. Rene Guenon, a French Orientalist, puts the distinction between metaphysical thought and philosophical thought as follows: 'Pure metaphysic necessarily excludes all systematization, because a system cannot avoid being a closed and limited conception, contained in its entirety within more or less narrowly defined boundaries, and as such is in no wise reconcilable with the universality of metaphysic; besides, a philosophical system is always the system of some particular person, that is to say, a construction, the value of which can only be purely individual. Furthermore, every system is necessarily erected upon some more or less special and relative foundation, being really nothing more than the development of a hypothesis, whereas metaphysic, which possesses the character of absolute certainty, cannot admit anything hypothetical.'[3] With Guenon's distinction between metaphysic and philosophy we do not agree, for it is possible to define philosophy in the same way as he has defined metaphysic. Nor do we endorse his view that there are no systems in Oriental thought. But what he says about Advaita or non-dualism is true. It eludes systematization. 'Non-dualism, such as we have described it in principle,' observes Guenon, 'is capable of

[1] See Introduction.
[2] See Commentary on the first Invocatory verse.
[3] *Introduction to the Study of the Hindu Doctrines* (Luzac & Co., London, 1945), p. 147.

immeasurably surpassing the scope of all philosophy [we would say, of all systematization], because it alone is genuinely and exclusively metaphysical in its essence, or in other words because it is an expression of the most essential and fundamental character of metaphysic itself.'[1]

It is only at the level of relativity (*vyavahara*) that there can be system or lack of it. The accounts of the world, soul and God, given by all, including the Advaitin, are but from this standpoint. The supreme truth (*paramartha*), however, which is the end of Advaita, cannot be caught within a system. Organisation and disorganisation are relevant to the realm of plurality; they have no meaning with reference to the non-dual reality. God, soul, and the world are spoken of as three from the standpoint of relativity which is also the standpoint of the ego; and it is the same ego that seeks to organise or systematize the three. The final truth is that they are not three. Hence, Sri Ramana says in this verse: Only one principle appears as three principles. *To say that the three principles ever remain as three principles is but so long as the egoity lasts.* Elsewhere he teaches: 'If the three, namely, the ego, world and God are considered to be distinct and separate from one another, they become illusory, like the silver in the mother-of-pearl. These three are really one and identical. They are the one Brahman or Atman.'[2]

Even to say that the three principles are one is not the highest truth. We say 'the Supreme is non-dual' in the language of duality. The plenary truth cannot, in fact, be expressed in words. So, the portion of the verse we are now commenting on may also be rendered thus: '*Only one principle appears as three principles. The three principles ever remain as three principles. To*

---

[1] *Introduction to the Study of the Hindu Doctrines*, p. 155.
[2] *Self-Realization*, p. 102.

say thus is but so long as the egoity lasts.' All words and thoughts,
all expositions and disputations are possible only when the ego
functions. To say that the real is one and non-dual is nearer the
truth than to say that it is many. But even to say that it is one is
to superimpose on it the category of number.

So, Sri Ramana says: *After the destruction of egoity, to remain
in one's own state is best.* The purpose of enquiry is to attain the
state of egolessness or mindlessness (*amani-bhava, amanasta*). The
ego, which is the first born of *avidya* (nescience), is what makes
for the distinction of 'I' and 'not-I' which in turn brings about
the entire host of finite experiences. To cease from involvement
in finitude, one must realize the state of non-mind. When this is
accomplished, there is nothing else to be done; one remains in
one's true nature which is the non-dual Self. This is what is known
as the natural (*sahaja*) state. Just as health which is one's normal
nature (*svasthya*) is regained on the removal of disease, which is
adventitious, through proper medicine, so release (*moksha*) which
is one's own true nature is attained[1] when nescience with its
product, the ego, is destroyed through wisdom (*jnana*). What is
figuratively called *attainment* here is but realization of the truth.

3. *'The world is real'; 'it is an illusory appearance', 'the world
is intelligent'; 'it is not'; 'the world is happiness'; 'it is not'; of what
use is it to argue thus? That state of egolessness is acceptable to all,
wherein leaving the world and understanding oneself, one is freed
from the notions of unity and duality.*

We have seen above that all expositions and disputations
are possible only when the ego functions. As an illustration,
reference is made in this verse to the disputes about the nature
of the world. There are various theories of the world. All of

---

[1] See Sureswara's *Sambandha-vartika*, v. 18.

them may be brought under one or the other of four categories which are: 'is', 'is not', 'both is and is not', and 'neither is nor is not'. The dialectic based on these four alternatives is known as *Chatuskoti* the logical quadruped. The primary alternatives, however, are the first two, 'is' and 'is not', the third affirms and the fourth denies the two together. The sevenfold mode of predications, called *saptabhangi-naya* in Jainism, is an elaboration of the *Chatuskoti*. The seven modes are: 'is', 'is not', 'is and is not', 'is inexpressible', 'is and is inexpressible', 'is not and is inexpressible', and 'is, is not and is inexpressible'. Of a thing, A for instance, we may say that it is; but it is as A and not as B. Yet it may become B sometime later or elsewhere in which case it ceases to be A. So we get the third mode of predication 'is and is not'. A is now; A is not afterwards. Or, A is here; A is not there. Such language is quite intelligible. But if affirmation and negation are made of a thing as conditioned by the same place and time, and in the same sense, the law of non-contradiction is violated. So what can be done under these circumstances is to make use of the fourth mode of predication. A neither is nor is not *i.e.*, A is inscrutable. The other modes of predication are combinations of the preceding ones. But here also it will be seen that the primary alternatives are 'is' and 'is not'. Sri Ramana points out in the present verse that disputes about the nature of the world result when the mind is moved by the two modes of affirmation and negation, 'is' and 'is not'.

'Is' and 'is not' are the forms in which a predication may be made. The attitude of world-affirmation adopts the form 'the world is', while that of world-negation takes the form 'the world is not'. But what is the content that is either affirmed or denied of the world? The answer is that the world is regarded either as having value or as not having value. The three aspects of value are reality (*sat*), intelligence (*chit*), and happiness (*ananda*). Reality-intelligence-happiness is value because it is the goal sought after by everyone; and its opposite, unreality-inertness-misery is valueless. This truth is superbly expressed in the *Brihadaranyaka Upanishad* in the form of a prayer:

> asato mā sad gamaya
> tamaso mā jyotir gamaya
> mṛityor mā'mṛutam gamaya!

> 'From the unreal, lead me to the real,
> From darkness, lead me to light,
> From death, lead me to immortality!'

Reality-intelligence-happiness is Brahman; unreality-inertness-misery is non-Brahman. Now, the question is: Is the world real, intelligent, and of the nature of happiness? Or, is it unreal, non-intelligent, and of the nature of misery? To say that the world is Brahman is ridiculous because the world of our experience is impermanent, for the major part unintelligent, and full of misery. To say that it is non-Brahman is unintelligible because there is nothing other than Brahman.

That is why the world and its cause, *maya*, are said to be *anirvachaniya*, indeterminable. *Maya* is neither real, nor unreal, nor both real and unreal. Therefore, it is indeterminable[1]. It may be urged by the critic that to say that *maya* is indeterminable is not satisfying to the inquiring mind, because it does not lead to an understanding of *maya's* nature. The reply is that *maya* cannot be understood by the intellect. Any defect (*dushana*) that may be

---

[1] See Sankara's *Sutra-bhashya*, I. iv. 3:
  avyakta hi sa maya: tattvanyatva-nirupanasyasakyatvat.

pointed out becomes an ornament (*bhushana*) to it. *Maya* is the expert *par excellence* in making apparently possible what is inherently impossible (*aghatita-ghatana-patiyasi*). The probing mind which is itself a product of *maya* has not the power to understand the nature of its parent. To the investigating intellect *maya* is a riddle.

With reference to Early Buddhism, an Italian scholar writes: 'The premise from which the Buddhist Doctrine of Awakening starts is the destruction of the demon of dialectics, the renunciation of the various constructions of thought, of speculation which is simply an expression of opinion, of the profusion of theories, which are projections of a fundamental restlessness and in which a mind that has not yet found in itself its own principle seeks for support'.[1] The same might be said of Advaita too. Ultimate truth is not attained through dialectic. If the *mere* intellect were to be the guide, then contradictory opinions may be held with equal weight and show of justification. 'Opinion, O disciples, is a disease,' declares the Buddha, 'Opinion is a tumour, opinion is a sore. He who has overcome all opinions, O disciples, is called a saint, one who knows.'[2] It is but an expression of opinion to say: 'The world is eternal', 'the world is not eternal', 'the world is finite', 'the world is infinite,'[3] etc. We do not arrive at the truth of the world by holding such opinions. So it is that Sri Ramana teaches that there is no use arguing, 'the world is real', 'the world is an illusory appearance', etc. And so Sri Sankara: 'The world of

---

[1] J. Evola, *The Doctrine of Awakening*, translated from Italian by H. E. Musson (Luzac & Co.. London, 1951), p. 47.

[2] *Majjhima-nikaya, CXL.*

[3] Cf. Kant's first antinomy: *Thesis* — The world has a beginning in time, and is also limited in regard to space. Therefore, it is finite. *Antithesis* — The world has no beginning in time; has no limits in space. In both these respects the world is infinite.

maya is indeterminable either as real or as unreal' (*tattva-anyatvabhyam anirvachaniya*).

That the world is indeterminable is from the standpoint of intellectual enquiry. There are two other standpoints — that of the worldly person and that of the seer who has realized the truth. The author of the *Panchadasi* refers to the threefold nature of *maya*, *i.e.*, the three ways in which *maya* appears thus:

tucchā' nirvacanīyā ca vāstavī ce 'ty asau tridhā,
jñeyā māyā tribhir bodhaiḥ śrautayauktika-laukikaiḥ.[1]

From the empirical standpoint the world is real; from the standpoint of the logical reasoning it is indeterminable, and from the standpoint of revealed scripture it is unreal. Why the world of *maya* is indeterminable so far as discursive reasoning goes, we have explained already. The man of the world believes as if the world is real. Such behaviour is what is called common sense. If he is asked how and why the world is real, he would not be able to give an answer.

The best that he could do, probably, to demonstrate the reality of the world is to behave in a way similar to what Dr. Johnson is reported to have done when he heard the theory of Bishop Berkeley that Matter does not exist, *viz.* to strike against the nearest stone. But there are some philosophers who put forward a common-sense theory — they are called realists — justifying belief in the reality of the world. They maintain that the world is 'apart from our consciousness, the same as it is for our consciousness',[2] as against the view of the subjective idealist that *to be is to be perceived*. To the man of common sense as well as to the common-sense philosopher, then, the world is real.

---

[1] VI, 130. Also *The Philosophy of Advaita*, p. 232.
[2] B. Bosanquet, *The Essentials of Logic* (Macmillan & Co. London, 1928), p. 8.

To the seer who has the plenary experience of Truth, the world is unreal. This is quite a different proposition from the mere argument that the world is unreal. To the one who sees and knows the truth as it is (*yatha-bhuta-jnana-darshana*), there is no world. He goes beyond the region of opinions. Even as the Buddha declared, he would say: 'Recognising the poverty of opinions, not adhering to any of them, seeking the truth, I saw.'[1] From the standpoint of the supreme Truth — if standpoint it may be called — the world is not. The linguistic expression of that experience is of the form 'the world is unreal'. A verse from the *Vivekachudamani* reads thus: '*Maya* and all *maya's* effects, from Mahat[2] to the physical body, are unreal and of the nature of not-Self; know then that these are like the mirage.'[3] Sri Ramana says: 'That is *maya* or illusion which makes one think and believe that that which is ever-present and all-pervasive, which is full of perfection and self-luminous and which is verily the Self, the core of one's Being as something non-existent and unreal. Conversely, that is *maya* which makes one think and believe as real and self-existent what is non-existent and unreal, namely the *jagat-jiva-para* (the world, the individual soul and God) which in all climes and throughout the ages have been declared an illusion.'[4]

An enquiry into the world of *maya* which we call science may add to our intellectual knowledge. It is, of course, necessary for world-welfare, though it often leads to large-scale destruction. But we do not become wise by an external analysis of the world. Narada of the Upanishadic age was a versatile genius. There was

---

[1] *Suttanipata*, IV, ix. 3.
[2] The first evolute of *prakriti*, according to Sankhya.
[3] Verse 25.
[4] *Spiritual Instruction* (Sri Ramanasramam, 4th Ed., 1948) p. 25

no science which he did not know, no art in which he was not an expert. Yet, he had to confess to Sage Sanatkumara that he was sorrow-stricken for lack of Self-knowledge[1]. The way to peace and blessedness, then, lies not in minute, and more minute study of the things of the world. That is why the Upanishads are indifferent to the doctrine of creation. While to a system like the Sankhya the order of creation is very important, and therefore with meticulous care the various stages in evolution are set forth therein, for Vedanta it does not matter whether all the elements appeared together or in succession, and whether the number of elements is three or five. The purport of the Upanishads is not to be found in the texts that speak about creation. The creation texts only serve the purpose, as Gaudapada observes, of introducing the texts which declare non-duality[2]. The world is not something to be clung on to, as if it were an end-in-itself. It must be crossed and superseded in order that we may arrive at Self-realization. The main purpose of the scriptures, says Sri Ramana, 'is to expose the illusory world as such and to reveal the unique Supreme Spirit as the only reality. They have built up the theory of creation with this sole end in view.'[3] Hence, he asks us to leave the world and understand the Self.

To understand the Self we must inquire into its nature. The path prescribed by Sri Ramana is the enquiry 'Who am I?' At first, it may appear strange that we should ask ourselves this question, for do we not know who we are? But, in fact, the many things with which we identify ourselves ordinarily turn out to be, on enquiry, not ourselves. The method that the master recommends is the surest way to Self-knowledge. Over and over

---

[1] *Chandogya*, VII,i.
[2] See *Gaudapada: A Study in Early Advaita*, pp. 112-4.
[3] *Self-Enquiry* (Sri Ramanasramam, 4th Ed., 1947), p. 35.

again he returns to it in his teachings. 'That which arises in the physical body as "I" is the mind. If one inquires whence the "I"-thought in the body arises in the first instance, it will be found that it is *Hridayam* or the Heart. That is the source and stay of the mind. Or again, even if one merely but continuously repeats to oneself inwardly "I-I" with the entire mind fixed thereon, that also leads one to the same source.... Since every other thought can occur only after the rise of the "I"-thought and since the mind is nothing but a bundle of thoughts, it is only through the enquiry "Who am I?" that the mind subsides. Moreover, the integral "I"-thought, implicit in such enquiry, having destroyed all other thoughts, gets finally destroyed or consumed, even like the stick used for stirring the burning funeral pyre gets consumed.'[1]

The state in which the mind has found its resolution is the state of egolessness which, Sri Ramana says, is acceptable to all. There one is free from the notions of unity and duality because there is no reckoner to count, nor anything that could be counted.

4. If oneself be with form, the world and the Supreme (viz. God) will be so (i.e. with form). If one be without form, who will see the form of those, and how? Verily, oneself is the Eye, the Endless Eye!

One of the modes of Self-enquiry is indicated in this verse. The Self is the centre of all things whether one recognises it or not. One may appear to deem some particular things or individual, such as wealth, a country, wife, son, etc., as supremely important. But on analysis it will be found that one is attached to them because they subserve the purposes of the Self. That is what Yajnavalkya taught his wife, Maitreyi. 'Not for the love of

---

[1] *Who Am I?* (Sri Ramanasramam, 7th Ed., 1948). pp. 10-12.

all is all dear, but for the love of the Self is all dear.' 'Lo, it is, verily, the Self that is to be seen, that is to be heard of, that is to be thought about, that is to be meditated on. Lo, Maitreyi, indeed by the sight of the Self, by its being heard of, by its being thought about, by its being known, all this becomes known.'[1] 'The Self is dearer than the son, dearer than wealth, dearer than everything else, and is innermost.'[2]

Advaita should not be confused with subjective idealism. The Self of which it speaks is not the individual soul or ego, the subject as against the object. If subjectivist arguments are pressed into service sometimes by Advaitins, it is for the purpose of refuting realism. In order to show the untenability of the views of those who seek to maintain the reality of external objects, the arguments of the Vijnanavadins are employed. The procedure here followed is similar to that adopted by Western absolutists in their criticism of the realistic doctrines. Subjectivist reasoning is advanced only to overthrow realism[3]. Occasionally an Advaita teacher may lean on the subjectivist mode of exposition in order to make his disciple understand him. Bharatitirtha, for instance, declares that the Self which is of one consistency of intelligence is single and that all jivas are posited by nescience; and when asked as to whose self this is, he replies, 'It is the real Self of you who thus ask me.'[4] The ultimate reality which is the Self, according to Advaita, however, is not the finite knower as against the plurality of known objects; it is the infinite consciousness in and for which there are no such distinctions as 'inside' and 'outside'.

This first line of the present verse in *Ulladu Narpadu* shows how the realist has really no answer to subjectivism. If we want

[1] *Brihadaranyaka*, II, iv, 5 and IV, v, 6.
[2] *Brihadaranyaka*, I, iv, 8.
[3] See *Gaudapada: A Study in Early Advaita*, p. 198.
[4] See *The Philosophy of Advaita*, p. 212.

to believe in the independent existence of an external world —
that is what the realist purports to do — we should first mark
ourselves off from the rest of the universe and identify ourselves
with our bodies. In order to assign a form to the world and to
God we ourselves must assume a form. The formed nature of
the world and of God depends upon our own form. We cannot
get at them except through our minds; and our minds are our
bodies. If one were to argue that, apart from ourselves and our
ideas, of nothing could one be certain, we shall find no way of
refuting his arguments, should we occupy the realist position.
The absurdity of subjectivism does not lie in its denial of the
existence of an independent world, but in its inadequate
conception of the Self as a finite mind. It is only when the Self
is regarded as the limitless spirit that it is easy to see how all the
things that we experience should owe their existence to it. Nay,
it is one and the same Self that appears as the multiple universe.

Someone asked a Zen master, 'How can we transform
mountains, rivers, and the great earth, and reduce them into
this Self?'

Replied the master, 'How can we transfer this Self and turn
it into mountains, rivers and the great earth?'[1]

Yes, the one becoming the many is a mystery, *maya*. There is
no other source possible for the universe except the Self. Hence, in
many a text of the Upanishads the origin of the world is traced to
the Self, Atman-Brahman. In a passage of the *Brihadaranyaka*, it is
stated that the Self, having become differentiated into name and
form, entered into the differentiations up to nail-tips as it were, like
a sword that fits its sheath or like fire that resides in its source.
Ordinarily, the Self is not recognised because it is mistaken for one

---

[1] See D. T. Suzuki, *Living by Zen* (Rider, 1950), p. 29.

of its aspects and is thus incomplete (*akritsna*). When it performs
the function of living, it is called the vital force; when it speaks, the
organ of speech; when it sees, the eyes; when it hears, the ear; and
when it thinks, the mind. These are but its names according to its
various functions. The Self is that in which all these are unified. It is
the Self that should be sought after and meditated on[1].

The Upanishad passage just cited is typical of all creation
texts. Two points may here be noted: (1) The Self is the sole
ground of the world. (2) It is not the purpose of Scripture to
teach creation. In fact, there is no real becoming. Creation is
mentioned only as an introduction to the realization of the truth
of non-duality. Explaining the latter point, Acharya Sankara says:
'The texts that speak of origination, entry, sustentation, and
destruction, are for the sake of the realization (of the Self); for
realization is declared to be the human goal.'[2]

It is for teaching the same truth, *viz.*, the non-duality of
the Self, that Sri Ramana says in the present verse: 'If oneself be
with form the world and the supreme (*viz.*, God) will be so
(*i.e.*, with form).' No one need be alarmed at the declaration
that the form of God depends upon our form. It is not stated
that God is dependent on the individual souls, that the Creator
is sustained by his creatures. All that is claimed here is that the
form we attribute to God is conditioned by our limitations. We
may think of God's omniscience and omnipotence. Even then
we are limiting his being. That is why candid theists like William
James and James Ward say that God too is finite, *primus inter
pares*, one of the eaches, or our Big Brother. This only shows
that all conceptions of God are bound to be unsatisfactory,

[1] *Brihadaranyaka*, I, iv, 7.
[2] *Brihadaranyaka*, Sankara's Commentary, Mem. Ed., Vol. 8, p. 102.

although they may be useful as props in our pilgrimage to truth. Through form we have to rise to the formless, where there is no duality, no division.

Even in our daily experience of sleep we see all forms vanishing, all names dissolving. Because in that experience the mind disappears in its cause which is *maya*, there is no duality of subject and object, of the seer and the seen. In sleep one is not conscious of what is without or what is within. The very notions of 'without' and 'within' have no meaning then. The Self is beyond desires, free from evil, and fearless. All empirical distinctions cease in the state of sleep. The Self remains relationless. 'There a father becomes not a father; a mother, not a mother; the worlds, not the worlds; the Gods, not the Gods; the Vedas, not the Vedas. There a thief becomes not a thief; the destroyer of an embryo, not the destroyer of an embryo; a *Chandala* is not a *Chandala*; a *Paulkasa* is not a *Paulkasa*; a mendicant is not a mendicant; an ascetic is not an ascetic. He is not accompanied by good, he is not accompanied by evil, for then he has crossed all sorrows of the heart.'[1] The Self is void of form in sleep, and so for it there is neither the world nor God. 'If one be without form, who will see the form of those, and how? Without the eye, is there sight?'

The experience of sleep is clear evidence to show that the Self is pure consciousness without involving a split into the seer and the seen. In sleep there is loss only of objective consciousness. Consciousness *per se* neither rises nor sets. It is ever self-luminous. Only in sleep ignorance persists, and so one returns to the world of duality. The final goal is to realize the non-dual reality without

---

[1] *Brihadaranyaka*, IV, iii, 22; see also *Gaudapada: A Study in Early Advaita*, pp. 93-94.

the veil of ignorance. In that ultimate experience, nothing else shines but the Self. 'Verily, oneself is the Eye, the endless Eye!'

5. The body is in the form of five sheaths; so, all the five are implied in the term 'body'. Apart from the body, is there a world? Say, are there people who, without body, have seen the world?

In the fourth verse it was shown that it is because we consider ourselves to be with form that we assign form to the world and God. We fence ourselves in; therefore, we fence the rest of the universe out. It is our bodies, then, that draw the dividing line. Usually, the term 'body' with its equivalents '*deha*', '*sarira*', etc., is used to denote the physical body. But strictly speaking, the entire psycho-physical organism is 'body'. Nay, even more; for the term includes the cause of our embodiment, which is *avidya* or nescience.

In Vedanta we hear of the division of 'body' into five sheaths (*kosha*). The *locus classicus* of this doctrine is in the *Taittiriya Upanishad*. In the chapter entitled 'Brahmananda', the Upanishad draws a picture, as it were, of five men one within the other, and all veiling the true Self. The five men are the five sheaths, each with a head, limbs, trunk, and support. As we go from the outermost to the inner forms, we get nearer the truth. Each outer stands to the inner in the relation of the filled to the filler. By the inner is the outer filled (*tena esa purnah*). In the next chapter of the *Taittiriya*, the story is told of Bhrigu's enquiry into the nature of Brahman. Being instructed by his father Varuna that Brahman is that whence all beings are born, wherein having been born they reside, and whereunto they return at the end, the boy makes his adventure in the realm of truth. He comes across the five sheaths, one by one, each time thinking that the sheath he is faced with is the reality, and each time going beyond, not being satisfied with his own discovery, till he arrives at the final truth that Bliss is Brahman.

The sheaths (*kosha*) are so called because they veil the Self, hiding it from our view. The five sheaths are: *annamaya, pranamaya, manomaya, vijnanamaya* and *anandamaya*. *Annamaya* is the sheath made of food, the physical body. Its constituents are the quintuplicated (*pancikrita*) elements, *i.e.* elements, not in their pure form, but in their varying grades of mixture. Of the same stuff as the physical body are the things of the experienced world made. *Pranamaya* is the vital sheath; it is that which makes for life, and its expression is the breath. On account of its five functions, the breath receives five names; *prana*, that which goes forward; *apana*, that which goes down; *vyana*, that which goes in all directions; *udana*, that which goes upward; *samana*, that which equalizes what is eaten or drunk. All the five are collectively referred to by the first name, *viz.*, *prana*. The *pranas* are said to be the products of the *rajas* aspect of the pure (non-quintuplicated) elements. To the sheath of *prana* belong also the five organs of action (*karmendriya*) — those of speech, · grasping, locomotion, excretion and generation. *Manomaya* is the sheath of consciousness. Desiring and doubting are the functions of *manas*. It arises out of the *sattva* phase of the pure elements. Its channels are the five organs of knowledge (*jnanendriya*) — those of hearing, touch, sight, taste and smell. *Vijnanamaya* is the sheath of self-consciousness; it is what is called *buddhi*, the agent of actions and the enjoyer of the fruit of actions. It is the empirical soul migrating from one physical body into another. *Anandamaya* is the sheath of bliss. It is not the original bliss which is Brahman. It is pseudo-bliss, and is the root-cause of transmigration. *Anandamaya* is another name for ignorance (*ajnana*) or nescience (*avidya*).

The five sheaths may also be rearranged into three bodies. *Annamaya* is the gross body (*sthula-sarira*). The next three, *pranamaya, manomaya* and *vijnanamaya*, constitute the subtle body (*sukshma-sarira*). And, *anandamaya* is the causal body (*karana-sarira*).

It is as endowed with these five sheaths or three bodies that we experience the external world in the state of waking. In dream-experience, the gross body does not function, but the other two bodies are active. While the wakeful enjoyments are gross, those pertaining to dreams are subtle. In deep sleep we experience neither the gross objects of the world without nor the subtle objects of the world within. But the causal body, *viz.*, nescience, persists. And, it is on account of this that we dream and become awake again.

So, as Sri Ramana teaches in the present verse, there is no world without body; and the kind of world depends on the type of body that is dominant for the time being. Speaking of time, we must add that even time varies in accordance with the state of experience. So do the nature of space and the principle of causation. Without the conditions of space, time and cause, there is no world. In the absence of these conditions, no one can experience a world.

6. *The world is of the form of the five (types of) sense-objects, and nothing else. Those fivefold sense-objects are the spheres of the five sense-organs. Since the one mind understands the world through the channels of the five sense-organs, say, is there a world other than the mind?*

What was taught in the previous verse is continued here. The world is an object of experience to the experiencing mind. The mind experiences the world by flowing along the sense-channels which are five in number. These are called the five cognitive sense-organs (*jnanendriya*): hearing, touch, colour, taste and smell. They are located in the various parts of the physical body, *viz.*, the ears, skin, eyes, tongue, and nose, respectively. The world of our experience consists of the objects of these sense-organs. The structure of the world, then, is correlative to the constitution of the senses. If the world of things has sounds, colours, etc., it is because we have ears, eyes, etc. What the world is apart from sounds, colours, etc., and whether there is such a world, we cannot say, and have no way of knowing.

We have to go even deeper than the sense-organs. The organs do not understand; they merely convey their respective objects to the mind. Without the mind, no objective knowledge is possible. One of the Upanishadic texts explains how the mind is central in all knowing. 'I was absent-minded, I did not see it', 'I was absent-minded, I did not hear it', thus says a person who was inattentive to things given to his senses. So, it is not simply through the sense that one experiences. It is through the mind that one sees and hears. The mind takes myriad forms, and fulfils a variety of functions. As the Upanishad puts it, 'Desire, deliberation, doubt, faith, lack of faith, patience, impatience, shame, intelligence and fear — all these are but mind.'[1]

Without the mind, then, there is no objective experience. Is there a world, asks Sri Ramana, other than the mind?

Here, again, we must note that it is not a brand of subjectivism that is taught by the Master. What is important to be borne in mind is the method of enquiry which proceeds from the outer to the inner, from the gross to the subtle. From the standpoint of the ultimate reality, there is neither outer nor inner, nothing gross and nothing subtle. But we have to advance from where we are. We

---

[1] *Brihadaranyaka*, I, v, 3.

habitually reside in the outer objects, in our bodies, senses and minds. In order to get to the Self, we have to withdraw from these in succession. This mode of approach is made clear, and its objective set forth in several Upanishads. The *Katha*, for instance, says: 'Superior to the senses are the subtle essences; superior to the subtle essences is the mind; superior to the mind is the intellect; superior to the intellect is Hiranyagarbha; superior to Hiranyagarbha is the unmanifest (*avyakta*); superior to the unmanifest is the Self (*purusha*); superior to the Self there is nothing whatever. That is the goal. That is the final destination.'[1] We have an echo of this teaching in the *Bhagavad Gita*: 'The senses are high, they say; higher than the senses is the mind; higher still than the mind is the intellect; and what is higher than the intellect is He.'[2]

Cosmologically, the Advaitin would make a distinction between cosmic creation and individual creation. As the author of the *Panchadasi* puts it, 'The universe has its origination in Isvara's contemplation and finds its completion in the production of jiva-hood. Of the so-called external world of the living and the non-living, God is the creator. Of the internal world of transmigratory existence which begins in the state of waking and ends in release, the Jiva is the author. The individual soul, thus, is the progenitor of its own microcosmic world.'

iksanādi-praveśāntā-srstir īśena kalpitā,

jāgradādi-vimoksāntah samsāro jīvakalpitah.[3]

Where it is said that the Mind is the cause of the world, what is meant is the cosmic Mind, and not the individual mind. It is in this sense that Gaudapada traces everything to *chitta*.

---

[1] *Katha*, III, 10,11.
[2] *Gita*, iii, 42.
[3] *Panchadasi*, vii, 4; see *The Philosophy of Advaita*, pp. 207, 208.

citta-spanditam evedam grāhya-grāhakavad-dvayam,
cittam nirviṣayam nityam asaṅgam tena kīrtitam.

'This world of duality, characterized by apprehended objects and apprehending minds, is set in motion by *chitta* alone. The *chitta* is without any object (as opposed to or different from it). Hence it is declared to be eternal and unattached.'[1]

7. Although the world and its awareness rise and set as one, it is by the awareness that the world shines. The Whole, wherefrom the world and its awareness rise and wherein they set, but which shines without rising and setting — that alone is the real.

The world of matter is inert and unintelligent (*achit*), and requires to be illuminated by a mind. Apart from a knowing mind, the world is not given in experience. To experience it is to know it. Thus, the objective world and its awareness are correlates. They appear and disappear together. The togetherness of the object and its awareness is recognised by the Vijnanavadin (the Bauddha subjectivist) too. But he argues that, because the two are always presented together, they are identical. Blue and its cognition are non-different, says he, as they are invariably together[2].

In Advaita, however, a difference is made, from the empirical standpoint, between awareness and its object. The mind or psychosis apprehends the object. It is true that the two rise and set together. In waking and dreaming there is the objective world as well as the seeing mind. Yes, in dreaming too there is a world of objects, and it is objectively experienced in that state. In deep sleep there is neither the world nor the mind. Sleep is defined in the *Mandukya* as the state wherein

---

[1] *Mandukya-karika*, IV, 72.
[2] *Sahopalambha-niyamad abhedo nila-tad-dhiyoh*

one does not desire any objects nor see any dream[1]. In the absence of the mind there, no objective experience is observed. So, it is clear that there is an invariable relation between mind and object. Yet, the difference between them is that the mind is the apprehender whereas the object is the apprehended. It is by the mind's light that the world shines.

The mind, however, has no light of its own. It too, like the object, is inert. But while it is capable of reflecting the light of intelligence which is the Self, the object is not. In the 'Kutastha-dipa' of *Panchadasi*, the object is compared to a plastered wall and the mind to a mirror set therein[2]. The mirror illumines the wall by the reflected rays of the sun. Similarly, the mind knows the object, being endowed with the reflection of intelligence.

It is the Self alone that is self-luminous. It neither rises nor sets.

nodeti nāstam ety ekā samvideṣā svayam-prabhā.

'It does not rise, nor does it set — this consciousness which is one and self-luminous.'[3] In a well-known context, the *Panchadasi* likens the Self to the lamp set on a stage. The lamp gives light to the manager of the drama, to the actors and to the audience without any distinction; and it shines even when the theatre is empty. Similarly, the Self which is the witness-intelligence (*saksi-chaitanya*) manifests egoity, the intellect and the objects, and continues to shine even when they are non-existent. The Self is the source of all light. The sense of egoity may be compared to the stage-manager, the intellect to the danseuse, and the objects to the audience; and the various sense-organs are the auxiliaries which aid the actress. All these are

---

[1] *Mandukya*, 5.
[2] *Panchadasi*, viii, 1-3.
[3] *Ibid*, i, 7.

illumined without distinction by the Witness-Self. Just as the lamp on the dramatic stage shines without moving and without being affected by the movements of the actors and the audience, even so the Self which is permanent and unchanging manifests all things both within and without[1].

'Light' is a favourite symbol with the ancients for indicating the nature of the Absolute. We often speak of the 'light' or 'torch' of knowledge. The 'knowledge of the mind' with which we are mostly acquainted is dependent knowledge. It is contingent and fugitive. It is *knowledge-of* and requires to be hyphenated with the self on the one hand and the object on the other. The Self is *knowledge-as* in the sense that its very nature is knowledge. *Prajnanam brahma*, the Absolute is awareness[2]. It is pure unmixed consciousness (*suddha-chinmatram*). One of the conversations between Janaka and Yajnavalkya, as recorded in the Brihadaranyaka,[3] relates to the question of light. The king asked, 'What light does a person here have?' 'He has the light of the sun, O king,' replied the Sage, 'for with the sun, indeed, as his light, one sits, moves about, does his work and returns.' The royal pupil, however, was not thus to be silenced. When the sun has set, what happens? The moon takes the place of the sun. In the absence of the moon? Fire becomes the light for man. When fire has gone out, what serves as man's light? Speech. And when speech is hushed, what light does a person have here? The final reply Yajnavalkya gave was: 'The Self (Atman), indeed, is his light; for with the Self, verily, as his light, one sits, moves about, does his work and returns.' And when asked, 'Which is the Self?', he said, 'The person here who among the senses is made of

---

[1] *Panchadasi*, x, 11-15; see also *The Philosophy of Advaita*, p. 187.
[2] *Ait.*, iii, 3.
[3] *Brh.*, IV, iii.

knowledge (*vijnanamayah*), who is the light in the heart (*hrdyantarjyotih*). Being the same, he goes along both worlds, seeming to think, seeming to move about; for, falling asleep, he transcends this world and the forms of death.'

In the *Kathopanishad* there is a verse which says,

na tatra sūryo bhāti na candra-tārakam
nemā vidyuto bhānti kuttoyam agniḥ,
tam eva bhāntam anubhāti sarvam
tasya bhāsā sarvam idam vibhāti.

'Not there does the sun shine, nor the moon and stars; these lightnings shine not; how can this fire (shine)? After Him, as He shines, everything shines; with His light, all this is illumined[1]. The same truth is taught in the *Bhagavad Gita*. 'That, the sun does not illumine, nor the moon nor fire. Attaining which one does not return, that abode supreme is Mine.'[2]

It is this ancient truth that Sri Ramana declares when he says that the Self is that 'wherefrom the world and its awareness rise and wherein they set, which but shines without rising and setting — that alone is the real.' The real Self is the 'Whole', the 'Full' (*purnam*). In the language of the mathematics of infinity, Scripture says:

pūrṇam adaḥ pūrṇam idam
pūrṇāt pūrṇam udacyate
pūrṇasya pūrṇam ādāya
pūrṇamevāvaśiṣyate.

'That is full, this is full; from the full the full arises; taking away the full from the full, the full alone remains.'

[1] *Katha*, II, ii, 15.
[2] *Gita*, xv, 6.

8. Under whatever name and form the omnipresent nameless and formless reality is worshipped, that is only a door to realization. Understanding one's own truth in the truth of that true reality, and being one with it, having been resolved into it, is true seeing. Thus should you know.

The reality which was described as the 'Whole' in the previous verse is the non-dual spirit. Other than it there is nothing real. It has no name and no form; for, all that has a name and a form is limited and finite. Even such expressions, as 'self' and 'spirit' are only symbols indirectly indicative of the true nature of the supreme reality. Even to say that it is non-dual, we have to superimpose the category of number on it. In the actual realization of its nature, words and thoughts cease. In stillness it is known as one's being. Thither mind and speech do not go. Hence it is that the absolute experience is said to be ineffable. So long as the individuality of the individual remains, that experience is not to be had. One cannot stand as an ego apart from the infinite Spirit and enjoy it. That is why the Lord of the *Gita* declares that the way of the unmanifest is difficult for those who are attached to their bodies.

It is in order to enable one to eventually get to the Absolute that the path of theism has been designed. The omnipresent nameless and formless reality is assigned name and form. This has inevitably to be so because we imagine ourselves to be possessed of a name and a form. So long as we are limited, our conceptions of the ultimate reality are bound to be limited. So long as we think we are persons, we have to ascribe personality to God. So long as we are endowed with characteristics, we must needs attribute characteristics to the Deity. Only we believe that the all-good God cannot be the home of despicable qualities (*heyaguna*). All his attributes are auspicious; there is no trace of evil in him. That is why he is worshipful, the lord worthy of veneration.

There are two types of theism, one which is fanatical and the other which seeks to be all-inclusive, corresponding to what philosophers of religion call the stages of national religion and universal religion. The fanatical type of theism urges that its conception of God alone is true, and that the other faiths are false. Each of the proselytizing religions believes that salvation lies through it alone. The slogan for the protagonists of conversion is: 'Either come to our fold or be damned.' Some followers of certain Hindu cults, it is true, have held fanatical views. The rivalry especially between the Saiva and the Vaisnavas is classical. And, in the medieval times, there were clashes among Jainism, Buddhism and the cults of Siva and Vishnu. But in spite of such occasional manifestations of discord and strife, Hinduism, on the whole, has stood for spiritual peace. It is the type of universal theism that is more in accord with its spirit. Probably the earliest declaration on record of universalism in faith is the *mantra* of the *Rig-veda* which says:

ekaṁ sad viprā bahudhā vadanti,
agniṁ yamaṁ mātariśvānam āhuḥ.

'Reality is one, though sages call it variously as Agni, Yama, and Matarisvan.'

In two well-known verses of the *Gita*, Sri Krishna proclaims the charter of freedom in worship:

yo yo yām yām tanuṁ bhaktaḥ
    śraddhayārcitum icchati,
tasya tasyācalaṁ śraddhām tām eva
    vidadhāmy aham.   (vii, 21)
ye yathā māṁ prapadyante tāms tathaiva
    bhajāmy aham,
mama vartmānuvartante manuṣyāḥ
    pārtha sarvaśāḥ. (iv, 11)

'Whatever be the form of God a devotee desires to worship with faith, I confirm him even in that unshakeable faith.' 'Whatever be the path in which people seek Me, even so do I bless them. It is My path, O Arjuna, that people pursue in all manner of ways.'

In one of the many similes given by Sri Ramakrishna the religions are compared to the *ghats* that lead to the Ganges. The unique mission which he came to fulfil was to show to a sceptical world that the various faiths were but ways to realize the same truth. Truth does not become different when you change the name. Water is water whether you call it *pani* or *jala*. If only the theologians cared for the content of their respective revelations without laying too much stress on the accidental features of these revelations, they would know that at the basis of the religions, there is One Religion. All the books declare that God is omnipresent, that He is the source of the world and its goal as well. What matters, then, if He be named *Iswara* or *Allah*? And so, Sri Ramana says in the present verse that under whatever name and form the omnipresent nameless and formless Reality is worshipped, that is a door to realization.

But mark, the Sage declares that that is *only* a door to realization! So long as there is difference — even the least — there is not the plenary realization. One has to transcend even the worshipper-worshipped relation. The highest reality is not to be characterized as this or that. It is not a God standing over against us. It is not the Other holding sway in some far off region. It is not this that is worshipped here, says the Upanishad. Brahman is not that which is apprehended by the sense organs and the mind; it is that which impels these to function. He who thinks, 'I am different, Brahman is different' does not know. He who says that he 'sees' God does not truly see. As the *Brihadaranyaka* puts it: 'Where there is duality, as it were, there one sees another, one smells another, one tastes another, one speaks to another, one hears another, one thinks of another, one touches another, one understands another. Where, however, everything has become just one's own Self, then whereby and whom would one see, whereby and whom would one smell, whereby and whom would one taste, whereby and to whom would one speak, whereby and whom would one hear, whereby and of whom would one think, whereby and whom would one touch, whereby and whom would one understand? He by whom one understands all this, whereby would one understand him? That Self is not this, it is not that (*neti, neti*). It is ungraspable, for it cannot be grasped; indestructible for it cannot be destroyed; unsticking, for it does not stick; is unbound, does not tremble, is not injured. Lo, whereby would one understand the understander?' (IV, v, 14).

True understanding, then, lies in realizing truth of identity or non-difference. As Sri Ramana says, one should understand one's own truth in the truth of that true reality, and be one with it, having been resolved into it. That is true seeing.

9. The dyads and the triads always subsist on the basis of the One. If one sees in one's heart as to what that One is, those (viz, the dyads, etc.), will disappear. They that see (thus) are the truth-seers; they are not perturbed. Thus should you see.

We have already seen that true understanding consists in realizing the truth of the non-dual Spirit. The vision of plurality is due to nescience, whereas the perception of unity is wisdom. But for the One, the Many will have no basis at all; even as, where there is no rope, the appearances of serpent, garland, streak of water, etc., would be impossible. The so-called modifications are mere names, given rise to by speech, says Scripture, what is real is the ground, even as clay is with reference to pots, pitchers, pans, etc.,

vācārambhaṇam vikāro nāmadheyam,
mṛittikety eva satyam.

It is true that it is not possible to explain how the One became the Many; for, the very concept of 'becoming' is riddled with contradictions. The purpose, however, of the Many is to lead us to the One. It is only when we are blind to this purpose that the Many weighs us down, and we get lost, as it were, without a proper sense of direction. But if we inquire into the meaning of the Many, we shall surely arrive at the One.

The very fact that we classify things and group them into kinds shows that the mere particular does not satisfy us. One of the usual modes of holding things together is by pairing them. Life and death, spirit and non-spirit, day and night, cold and heat are some of the well-known dyads. It is interesting to note that one of the philosophical hymns of the *Rig-veda* known as the *Nasadiya-sukta* names several pairs of categories and says that the one reality is not to be identified with either member of each pair. The pairs mentioned in the hymn are: being/non-being, death/deathlessness, night/day, and mass/energy. The most universally accepted division of reality is into spirit and matter. The primary categories, according to Jainism, are *jiva* and *ajiva*, soul and non-soul. Rene Descartes divided substance into *res cogitans* and *res extensa*, thinking substance and extended substance. The epistemological pair corresponding to this division consists of the knower and the known, the seer and the seen.

Some philosophers prefer the triadic process to the division by dichotomy. An analysis of the constitution of the world made the Sankhyas conceive of *prakriti* as a composite of three *gunas*,

viz., *sattva, rajas* and *tamas*. In the early Upanishads we read of
the process of triplication (*trivritkarana*) by means of which three
primary elements combine in the production of the world. The
Vedanta analyses the world into three categories, name (*nama*),
form (*rupa*), and action (*karma*). Epistemologically, there are
three factors involved in cognitive experience, *viz.*, cognizer
(*jnata*), cognized object (*jneya*) and cognition (*jnana*).

In whatever way one may divide the world, into two, three
or many, the basic reality, declares Sri Ramana, is one. The dyads,
triads, etc., subsist on the basis of the One. Without the unit or
unity, nothing can be numbered. Though we refer to the real as
one or non-dual only after superimposing thereon the category
of number, number one is primary while the other numbers are
secondary. Employing the analogies of fire and wind, the
Kathopanishad seeks to explain how the One became the Many,
as it were. 'As the one fire, having entered the world becomes
corresponding in form to every form, so the one inner Self of all
beings is corresponding in form to every form, and is yet outside.
As the one wind, having entered the world becomes
corresponding in form to every form, so the one inner Self of all
beings is corresponding in form to every form, and is yet outside.'
The Self is the ground of the world, and is not exhausted by it.
The one is immanent in the Many and yet transcends it.

The aim of the Indian philosophy is not merely to
appreciate intellectually the magnificence of the One, but to
realize it in immediate experience. In other words, it has to be
apprehended not only by the mind but also in the heart. In the
language of the *Katha*, the Self is to be framed by the heart, by
the thought, by the mind. So Sri Ramana says that the One is to
be seen in one's heart. This is true seeing or seeing the truth.
Those who see the truth thus are not perturbed. Perturbation

results, only when one is lost in the maze of plurality. To the wise who have the vision of the One, there is no delusion, no sorrow.

10. There is no knowledge apart from ignorance; there is no ignorance apart from knowledge. To whom are that knowledge and that ignorance? The knowledge which knows thus the Self which is the ground principle is (true) knowledge.

It is usual to distinguish between science and superstition, knowledge and ignorance. But it is not difficult to realize that the two are relative and even complementary to each other. The history of science has been one of relentless struggle with ignorance and its brood — prejudice and superstition. But that history also reveals that the science of today may become the superstition of tomorrow. In primitive times people used to rely abjectly on the wizard and the magic-worker for their existence and knowledge. Today that reliance has been transferred to the scientist and technician. Though it is true that modern science and technology have mitigated human misery to some extent and added some comfort to human existence, it is irrational on our part to surrender ourselves to them in the hope that they will save us from all troubles, and that they will eradicate suffering and ignorance. The past record only shows that fresh troubles have been added and new types of ignorance too. To quote the words of a British scientist, Prof. A. V. Hill, "In fact, every technical advance, every scientific or medical discovery brought with it human problems to solve, moral, social, political or aesthetic. To imagine that scientific and technical progress alone can solve all the problems that beset mankind is to believe in magic, and magic of the unattractive kind that denies a place to the human spirit". Thus, it is clear that science does not mean omniscience. If the frontiers of knowledge are extended in one direction, the floods of ignorance invade in another. In fact, every new knowledge brings with it a new ignorance. As Sri Ramana says in the present verse. 'There is no knowledge apart from ignorance.'

Why is this so? Because our knowledge of objects is rooted in ignorance. True Knowledge is knowledge of the Self, what in our commentary on the previous verse was described as the vision of the One. All other knowledge is knowledge only in name. In the Upanishads, a distinction is made between two kinds of knowledge, the higher and the lower, *para vidya* and *apara vidya*. The higher knowledge is Self-knowledge. The lower knowledge is the knowledge of objects. This latter is impossible without *avidya* or nescience. *Avidya* performs a double function: it veils the real and projects the non-real world. These two aspects of *avidya* are called respectively *avarana* and *vikshepa*. It is the projected world that we come to know through the ordinary avenues of knowledge, such as perception, inference, etc. This knowledge which is graded as lower, is rooted in *avidya*. Hence, 'there is no knowledge apart from ignorance.' Sri Sankara observes in his commentary on the *Taittiriya Upanishad* thus:

nāmarūpa-pakṣasyaiva vidyāvidye,
na ātmādharmau ... te ca punar
nāmarūpe savitary ahorātre iva kalpite.

'Knowledge and ignorance belong to the realm of name and form; they are not the attributes of the Self....And, they — name and form — are imagined, even as day and night are with reference to the sun.'

Here the illustration of the sun is very apt. From the standpoint of the sun, there is no day and night. Yet, without reference to the sun, there is neither day nor night. It is from the point of view of the earth that day and night have meaning, and they are superimposed on the sun. Similarly, in the pure Self there is no knowledge and no ignorance. These are relevant only to finite intelligences. But these, again, acquire meaning as superimposed on the Self.

Just as there is no knowledge apart from ignorance, there is no ignorance apart from knowledge. The Self which is the absolute reality is of the nature of knowledge — knowledge, not in the sense of a transformation of the mind, but in the sense of unconditioned awareness. It is this awareness that is the basis of the primal ignorance called *avidya* or *maya*. Ignorance resides in the Self and obscures it. In the technical language of Vedanta, the Self is the *ashraya* (locus) as well as *vishaya* (content) of ignorance. Recalling his sleep-experience, a person says, 'I did not know anything then.' Now, the question is, how did he know that he did not know anything? Without awareness, non-knowledge of anything is not possible. In other words, without the basic awareness, non-knowledge or ignorance is not possible. Similarly, when one says to another, 'I do not know what is stated by you', that one's not knowing has its basis in awareness. In fact, it is this characteristic of ignorance that makes its removal possible. If there is no awareness of ignorance, ignorance cannot be removed.

What, then, is the way to the removal of ignorance? The answer is *para vidya*, the higher knowledge, which is defined in the Upanishad as that by which the Self is known. In the present verse, Sri Ramana teaches a method by means of which the Self could be known. We have already seen that without reference to the Self, knowledge and ignorance are void of meaning. The enquiry takes the form: To whom are knowledge and ignorance? What is their ground-principle? The basic awareness of both knowledge and ignorance is the true awareness. It is the Self which is pure consciousness (*prajnanam brahma*).

*11. Without knowing the knowing Self, to know what is other
— can it be knowledge, and not ignorance? When the Self, which is
the ground of knowledge and the other, is known, both the knowledge
and the ignorance will cease.*

(The topic of verse ten is continued in the next three verses.)
In every knowledge-situation, three factors, *triputi* are involved,
viz., the knower, the process of knowing and the object of
knowledge. The result of the process of knowing is called
knowledge. The Sanskrit terms for these four, are, respectively,
pramata, pramana, prameya and *pramiti.* When I see the yonder
hill, for instance, I am the cognizer, the process of cognizing is
visual perception and the object of cognition is the hill. What
results from this is the cognition of the hill. Similarly, when AB
infers the existence of fire on a particular hill on the perception of
smoke thereon, AB is the knower, the process of knowing is
inference, fire is the object of knowledge, and the resulting
experience is the inferential knowledge of fire. Thus in all such
knowledge, we know what is 'other' than the Self. For the sake of
convenience, we may call it 'objective' knowledge. By 'object' here,
we mean not only the things that exist outside our body, but also
the body and the contents of the mind as well. Ordinarily, it is
the knowledge of objects that is said to be knowledge. But, as was
shown in our commentary on the previous verse, this is not
knowledge at all. It is a play of ignorance. We are busy about all
things other than the Self, and by knowing them we imagine we
become wise. This imagination is absolutely wrong. Wisdom lies
not in acquiring information about the products of ignorance,
but in discovering the true nature of the Self which is the seat of
knowledge, nay knowledge itself. So, in the present verse it is
asked: 'Without knowing the knowing Self, to know what is other
— can it be knowledge and not ignorance?' The answer is implied

in the question. All 'objective' knowledge is ignorance, and not knowledge.

True knowledge, then, is the Self. But for the Self, the entire world will be blind. The light of the Self is required for illumining the presence as well as the absence of objects.

It is through our mind that we know objects. But the mind is inert. Its intelligence is borrowed from the Self. So, the Self is the ground of even objective knowledge. It is the ground of the ignorance of objects also. And, nescience (*avidya*) which is the root of relativity has its basis in the Self. Thus, the Self is the ultimate ground of knowledge and ignorance, of the appearance and disappearance of objects.

Here, it will be seen that the terms 'knowledge' and 'ignorance' are each of them, used in two different senses:

1. Absolute knowledge   = Self-knowledge.
2. Relative knowledge   = Knowledge of objects.
3. Metaphysical ignorance   = Nescience.
4. Mental ignorance   = Ignorance of objects.

1 is the ground of 3, and 3 is the cause of both 2 and 4. Thus we have in a descending order:

(a) Self (*Brahman-Atman*).
(b) Nescience (*maya-avidya*).
(c) Mind (*antahkarana-manas*).

Knowledge and ignorance, light and shade, oppress us, so long as we are denizens of the realm of mind. In the states of waking and dream, we are aware of certain objects and ignorant of others. We consort with the objects we experience, and lose ourselves in them. In deep sleep, the scene changes and the *dramatis personae* disappear. The Self is stripped pure; and yet nescience lingers. It is only when Self-knowledge dawns that all relativity ceases.

12. What is other than knowledge and ignorance — that is (true) knowledge. Objective knowledge cannot be true knowledge. Since the Self shines without there being anything else to know or to be known, it is knowledge; it is not nullity. Thus should you know.

Self-knowledge is true knowledge. It is other than objective knowledge and ignorance. The so-called knowledge of objects is not knowledge in the true sense of the term. Knowledge, to be knowledge, must be self-luminous. The Self alone is self-luminous. Hence it alone is true knowledge.

Anandabodha, a great teacher of Advaita, puts the case for the self-luminosity of the Self thus: The Self is self-luminous because it is not and cannot be manifested by anything else. Men recede from objects that are hurtful and approach those that are helpful. The knowledge that a particular object is either helpful or hurtful is dependent on its determinant, *viz.*, the luminosity of the Self, because it is a determinate light. And, this luminosity of the Self is dependent on nothing else, because while manifesting everything, it is not manifested by any other thing[1].

Chitsukhacharya, another eminent Advaitin, defines self-luminosity as the capability of being called immediate in empirical usage, while remaining at the same time a non-object of knowledge. The Self is not an object of cognition; yet it is fit to be called immediate. It is self-luminous because it is of the nature of experience or intelligence. What is not experience is not self-luminous, *e.g.*, a pot. All objects shine because of the luminosity of the Self. There is no light other than its own that can make the Self shine. Therefore, the Self is self-luminous[2].

---

[1] See the present writer's *The Philosophy of Advaita*, p. 136.
[2] *Ibid* ., p. 140 *et. seq.*

It is the same truth of self-luminosity that Sri Ramana teaches in the words: 'Since the Self shines without there being anything else to know or to be known, it is knowledge.' Other than the Self, there is nothing which knows, nor is there anything which is to be known. The Self is pure unconditioned awareness (*suddha-chinmatram*).

Some believe that, if the objects are denied reality, the Self would be reduced to a void (*sunya*). They accuse Advaita of affiliation with *Sunyavada*. But they are wrong. The Self is plenitude of being, and not nullity. While everything else may be denied, the Self cannot be denied. There cannot be limitless denial. The limit of denial is the Self. While the particular contents of awareness may be shown to be unreal or even non-existent, the awareness itself cannot be dispensed with. And, as has been stated already, the Self is awareness.

13. The Self alone is knowledge, truth. The knowledge of plurality is ignorance, illusion. That ignorance is not apart from the Self which is knowledge. The many ornaments are illusory. Say, do they exist apart from the gold which is real?

The non-dual Self is pure awareness; it is the supreme truth. Truth is that which is non-contradicted at any time, anywhere. It is unconditioned by space, time and causation. Judged by this test, the Self alone is truth. The pluralistic universe, on the contrary, is an illusory appearance. In the experience of sleep it is not seen. And, at the onset of knowledge, it vanishes. So, it cannot be true. The knowledge of what is not true is ignorance. But ignorance has no ontological status alongside or apart from the Self which is true knowledge. If it has to be located anywhere, it must lie in the Self. Just as the darkness present in a room obscures the room, the ignorance which is located in the Self veils it. If it be asked how the darkness of ignorance could reside in the self-luminous Self, we have no answer. From the standpoint of the absolute reality, there is no ignorance at all. It is only from the side of relativity that we can talk of ignorance. And all talk of ignorance is bound to be incoherent and illogical. For, incoherence and lack of logic are the very soul of ignorance (*maya*).

To illustrate the truth that the One alone is real and the Many illusory, an example is given. This occurs in the *Chandogya Upanishad* (VI, i), along with other examples. Just as various types of ornaments are wrought out of gold, so the plurality of things constituting the world is apparently produced from the one Self. Apart from gold there are no ornaments. Even so apart from the Self there is no world. When one understands gold, one understands everything that is made of gold. Similarly, when one knows the Self, one comprehends the world. The so-called effect is non-different from the cause. The other examples given in the *Upanishad* are: (1) one piece of clay and the things made of clay. (2) nail-scissors and iron products.

14. If the first person exists, then the second and the third persons will also exist. If, by an enquiry into the truth of the first person, the first person ceases, then the second and the third persons will (also) cease: and all will shine as one. The state of being so is one's true nature.

It was stated in verse nine that the dyads and triads always subsist on the basis of the one. In verses 10-13 one of the dyads consisting of knowledge and ignorance was examined, and it was shown that the Self is the basis thereof. The scope of the present verse is the triad of persons, first, second and third.

The first person 'I', the second person 'you' or 'thou' and the third person 'he', 'she' or 'it' constitute the triad of persons. Of these, the second and the third are dependent on the first. It is one's egoity that is referred to as 'I'. And it is as contrasted with the egoity that the other entities are characterised as 'you', 'he', 'she', or 'it'. Whether it is the 'I-thou' relation or the 'I-it' relation, it is clear that without the 'I' no relation is possible. The 'I' is the basis of the matrix of relations. All plurality then arises out of the 'I'. If the plurality must cease, the 'I' must cease. The way to the cessation of the 'I', as taught by Sri Ramana, is enquiry into the nature of the 'I'. Persistently ask yourself the question 'Who am I?' The final answer to that question will be the cessation of the 'I'-process. And when the 'I' ceases, the 'thou' and the 'it' will automatically cease, even as when the dreaming ego gets dissolved, all the dream-contents disappear.

It may be asked whether after this *hara-kiri* anything will be left over. Even the yogins have this apprehension, says Gaudapada, that after the 'I' goes nothing may remain. They are afraid of the 'nil'-end. But there is no ground for such fear. If the 'I' goes, the Self remains. The Self is the reality of 'I', 'thou', and 'it'. The expressions 'I my*self*', 'thou thy*self*', 'it it*self*', etc., show that the Self is the basis of 'I', 'thou', 'it', etc. So, when we catch hold of the 'I'-process by the tail, as it were, and trace it back to its root, what happens is that it gets resolved in the Self. In the place of the Many, we have the One shining of its own accord. That is one's true nature, because that One is oneself.

15. In relation to the present do the past and the future stand. Even they are present, while they last. The present is one alone. Without knowing the truth of the present, seeking to know the past and the future is like wanting to count without the unit, one.

Here is another triad, *viz.*, past, present and future. These are the conventional divisions of time, which, on analysis would be found to be meaningless. The part of time of which we are immediately aware is said to be the present. But the present that is experienced is not a point but a length of time. In it both past and future meet; and it is not possible to say where the one ends and the other begins. If time as past-present-future is analysed, there arises a host of contradictions which the ingenuity of the human intellect cannot quell. Past, present and future are evidently distinctions, and yet they cannot be distinguished. The past was present and the future will be present. Experience or awareness is always present. It is the 'ever-now' or eternity, whereon time as past-present-future is superimposed. He who hugs time, imagining it to be absolute, will come to no good. Time is transcended in the timeless; and the timeless is the basis of time. Trying to understand the time-process without recognising the timeless which is the 'Eternal Now' is like attempting to count without the unit of reckoning, which is 'One'.[1]

16. On enquiry, where is time and where is space, apart from us? If we are the bodies, we shall be involved in time and space. Are we the bodies? We are the same, now, then and ever; the same here, there and everywhere. Know this: We are; time and space are not; we are.

In the previous stanza it was shown that time is not real, and that on analysis it is found to be unintelligible. Here, in this stanza, space is added to time as the concept of something which is an illusory appearance. Space and time go together and must share the same fate. They have no independent status apart from the Self which is awareness. We have already seen that 'past' and 'future' have no meaning unrelated to the 'present'. Similarly, 'this side' and 'that side', 'above' and 'below', 'front' and 'back', 'near' and 'far' have no significance taken out of their relation to 'here'. And, when we inquire into the nature of the 'here', we realize its unintelligibility. 'Points' and 'instances' are

---

[1] See the present writer's *Time and the Timeless* (Principal Miller Lectures, 1953).

useful in what is called practical life. But once the light of intelligence is focused upon them, they vanish.

Space and time are sought to be determined with reference to the body — the physical frame — and the mind. Space positions such as 'right' and 'left', 'up' and 'down', etc., have a bearing to the body position at a given instant. 'Past', 'present' and 'future' are shifting distinctions in the mental stream. So, what is involved in space and time is the body (including mind). It is the body that changes and can be moved from place to place, not the Self.

The Self is unchanging, eternal, omnipresent. It is the same, now, then and ever; the same here, there and everywhere. The very first doctrine taught by Sri Krishna in the *Bhagavad Gita* relates to the eternity and all-pervasiveness of the Self. The Self can never be limited by space and time. It is the body that is so limited. Because we wrongly identify the Self with the body, we superimpose the limitations of the latter on the former. The truth, however, is that the Self is 'eternal, all-pervading, firm, unmoving and ancient' (*Gita*, ii, 24). So Sri Ramana declares in this verse: 'We are; time and space are not.' The plural 'we' does not mean that there is a real plurality of the selves. Since all teaching is for us, the teacher has to use the language that we can understand. When the Lord of the *Gita* says, 'Never was I not, nor thou, nor these kings. Never hereafter shall we all cease to exist.' He too employs the plural 'we'. As Sankara points out in his commentary on the *Gita*, the plural 'we' is in accordance with the difference of bodies, and not with a view to teach that there is a plurality of selves:

dehabhedānuvṛtyā bahuvacana
na ātmabhedābhiprāyeṇa.

17. To those who have not realized the Self and to those who have realized, the body is 'I'. To those who have not realized, the 'I' is only of the measure of the body. To those who have, within the body, realized the Self, the 'I' shines without limit. This is the difference between the two. Thus should you know.

When one begins to move on the path of enquiry, one distinguishes the Self from the not-Self. Discrimination between the eternal and the non-eternal (*nitya-'nitya-vastu-viveka*) is one of the prerequisites of the Vedanta-study. But when one completes the journey and gains the plenary wisdom, one realizes that the Self alone is, with naught besides. What is called 'not-Self' is an appearance of the Self and should be included herein. This is the distinction between the one who is ignorant and the one who has realized the truth; while the former mistakes the not-Self for the Self, the latter knows that the Self is all.

In the present verse, Sri Ramana contrasts the experience of the realized one with that of the person who is ignorant. Both refer to the body as 'I'. It is only the *sadhaka* that needs speak of the body as 'this'. The realized one need not have recourse to such a device. He may as well use the term 'I' with reference to the body. What, then, is the difference between him and the ignorant person? While the ignorant person limits the 'I' to the body, the realized one knows that the Self which is the meaning of 'I' has no limit at all. So, it is not wrong to say 'the body is "I"', because all, including the body must fall within the sphere of 'I'. But it is fallacious to convert this proposition simply and say 'the "I" is body.' The type of conversion that should be applied here is conversion *per accidens*. The legitimate converse of the proposition 'the body is "I"', 'is a part of "I", or an appearance of "I" is the body.' Those who are ignorant do not realize this truth. They think that the frontiers of the 'I' are the periphery of their body. Pointing to their body, they would say: 'I am this much alone and nothing beyond'; 'this is I, that is you and that other is it'. For those who have realized the truth, however, there is nothing but 'I' *viz.*, the Self. The Self shines without limit.

Self-realization comes to one the moment ignorance is dispelled. This need not wait till the body dies. *Moksha* is not something to be newly accomplished. It is not a post-mortem experience. It is the ever-accomplished end. Only ignorance or *avidya* stands as a veil between us and the truth. Once the veil is removed, there is no more bondage. Even while tenanting a body, one may succeed in tearing the veil and realizing the Self. Such a one is a *jivanmukta*, to whom the Self shines as the limitless reality.

18. To those who have not realized, as well as to those who have realized, the world is real. To those who have not realized, reality is of the measure of the world. The reality, according to those who have realized, is formless, and shines as the ground of the world. This is the difference between the two. Thus should you know.

What was said in the previous verse regarding the body is now stated with reference to the world. To the *jnani* as well as to the *ajnani* the world is real. But the difference is that, while to the former, reality is much more than the world, to the latter, the world is the only reality. Even empirical usage will bear out the truth of the *jnani's* experience. We say that the world is real and not that reality is the world. But the *ajnani's* belief in the sole reality of the world would imply the latter of the two propositions.

The world is called *prapancha* because it has five characteristics, *viz.*, existence (*asti*), manifestation (*bhati*), lovability (*priyam*), name (*nama*) and form (*rupa*). Of these, the last two vary from entity to entity. They are inconstant and are products of *maya*. It is these that the ignorant regard as the world. The first three constitute the essential nature of the Self which is existence-consciousness-bliss. The wise ones know that this is reality which is the basis of the world, and of which the world is an appearance. The *Drig-drisya-viveka* declares what has just now been explained in the following verse:

> asti bhāti priyaṁ rūpam
> nāma ce'ty amśa-pañcakam,
> ādya-trayaṁ brahma-rūpam
> jagad-rūpaṁ tato dvayam[1].

This, then, is the difference between the ignorant and the wise. To the ignorant the world is name and form, and beyond the collocation of names and forms nothing is real. To the wise, the reality is the formless ground of the world. The *Brahma-sutra* (I. i. 2) defines *Brahman* as that whence the world has its origin, etc.

> janmādy asya yataḥ.

In the *Taittiriya Upanishad*, Varuna teaches his son, Bhrigu; 'That from which all these beings arise, that by which having arisen they exist, and that into which at the end, they enter — that is *Brahman*.'

> yato vā imāni bhūtāni jāyante
> yena jātāni jīvanti, yat prayanty
> abhisaṁviśanti, tad brahma.

19. The dispute as to what wins, fate or free-will, is only for those who have not the knowledge of the ground of fate and free-will. Those who have

---
[1] See *The Philosophy of Advaita*, p. 116.

realized the peerless Self which is the ground of fate and free-will are free from them. Say, will they resort to them again?

The state of those who have realized the truth is made further clear in this stanza. All contradictions cease here; and there are no problems to be solved. As an illustration, the question of fate *versus* free-will is cited.

There is no problem in ethics which has been the subject of so much dispute as that of the freedom of the will. This has proved to be a veritable hornet's nest. The determinists and the indeterminists have waged battles royal on this issue, the former maintaining that man is completely a creature of circumstances, and the latter urging that he is the marker of his own destiny.

The various brands of Naturalism regard man as part of nature, as essentially the same in kind as any other species, subject to the same laws, behaving in the same way. The sense of freedom which he may feel sometimes is only imaginary and not real. The so-called moral behaviour of man is not different from, say, the falling of a stone or the flight of a bird in pursuit. The consistent naturalist who is a necessitarian or determinist thinks, therefore, that there is no meaning in the 'ought' of morality. Ethics is a natural science and not a normative study. Its task is to investigate what men do or tend to do, and not what they ought to do. To the evolutionary biologist, man is an item in the course of evolution, governed by the natural law of existence, survival and supercession. To the behaviouristic psychologist, he is a mechanism, though complicated, for receiving stimuli and responding to them. His brain thinks even as his liver secretes bile. To the dialectical materialist, man appears as a product of economic forces, shaped or mis-shaped by his material conditions, and acting according to set patterns, urged by the primary needs of living. Thus, all determinists are agreed in denying to man initiative and freedom and in converting him into a robot or automaton. He can take credit to no action of his; nor can he be blamed for any of his failings. He has no responsibility whatsoever. He is to be considered more a patient of external forces than an agent of actions.

There is a higher determinism which is that of the theologian, according to whom

'There is a divinity that shapes our ends,
Rough-hew them how we will.'

We are as nothing before the might and glory of God. Not a sparrow falleth without His consent. Our wills are ours, only to make them His. It is in vain that man sometimes attempts to get out of God's plan. He mistakenly thinks that he can make or mar his future. But one day or other he has to wake from this delusion, and realize that God is the sole impeller of all things and the undisputed architect of the world.

The indeterminists or libertarians who are mostly pluralists and personalists, will not brook the fettering of man's will either by nature or by God. Their main argument is that if man is not responsible for his actions and has no freedom to choose between alternative courses of conduct, he cannot be the subject of moral judgement, and there will be no distinction between good and evil. As Kant urged, there would be no meaning in an 'ought' if it were not accompanied by a 'can'.[1] If man cannot do what he ought to do, morality would become meaningless, and there could be neither praise nor blame for what one actually does. Weighing the *pros* and *cons* of the contending doctrines, William James states his conclusion thus: 'While I freely admit that the pluralism and restlessness (of a universe with freedom in it) are repugnant and irrational in a certain way, I find the alternative to them is irrational in a deeper way. The

---

[1] See J. S. Mackenzie, *A Manual of Ethics* (University Tutorial Press Ltd., London, 1929), p. 73.

indeterminism offends only the native absolutism of my intellect, an absolutism which, after all, perhaps, deserves to be snubbed and kept in check. But the determinism ... violates my sense of moral reality through and through.'[1] In order to safeguard the freedom of the individual, some of the modern pluralists even go to the extent of limiting the power of God. God, according to them, is one of the eaches, and not the Almighty. He is merciful, but not omnipotent.

There are some moralists who reject both determinism and indeterminism. Both freedom and necessity, they would say, are essential to morals. There is no unrestricted or unlimited freedom, nor is there absolute necessity. 'Necessity is the inseparable condition, or rather let us say, co-element of freedom. And without that co-element, thinking is as incapable of being understood as freedom, as walking is impossible without ground to tread on or flying without air to beat.'[2] Man is conditioned by what he has inherited. What he has inherited depends on his own past. But with this as his initial capital, he can build his future. A sculptor finds his material given. But how he shapes his material depends upon his own skill. Morality requires neither predestination nor indetermination, but self-determination.

It is in this sense that the *karma* doctrine is to be interpreted. *Karma* is not a relentless fate pushing man to a preordained destiny. It is what man has achieved in the past; and he is answerable to it. He has acquired also certain tendencies and dispositions which make him act in one way rather than in another. But he can change them in the present and shape his future according to his will.

---

[1] *The Will to Believe and Other Essays*, pp. 145-183. Quoted in James Seth A Study of Ethical Principles (William Blackwood. Edinburgh, 10th Ed. 1908), p. 373.

[2] *Mind*, O.S. Vol. v, p 252.

God in such a scheme would be the general ground for the operation of the law of *karma*. God or *daiva* is not opposed to human effort or *purusha-kara*. Both are necessary for making morality possible and yield its result. *Reader's Digest* (Sept. 1953) provides an interesting illustration: 'A widow, who had been left with six sons to bring up, was asked how she had managed to raise such exceptional sons alone and unaided, "It did take grit and grace", she said, "but I wasn't exactly unaided — the Good Lord helped me. Every night I knelt and told him I'd furnish the grit if He would furnish the grace."'

In the light of our discussion of the problem of fate versus freedom, let us understand Sri Ramana's solution. What is it that is said to be free or fettered in action? It is the will. Now, the will implies an ego that exercises the will. It is from the standpoint of the ego that the problem arises at all. If the ego is unobstructed in activity, it is believed to be free. If it is opposed by the non-ego either in the form of nature or in the form of God, and is conditioned thereby, obviously it cannot be free. The ethical 'ought' is meaningless without freedom. Yet the limited ego finds itself in chains. So long as we refuse to go beyond the level of the ego, the problem cannot be solved.

What, then, is the solution? Self-knowledge. The ground of the ego and the non-ego is the Self. It is the ground of fate and free-will. It is without peer because there is nothing besides it. It is the sphere of actionlessness. How, then, can there be the function of will? For those who have realized this truth, there is no problem to solve. Such considerations as 'This I have done'. 'This I have not done' do not arise in their case. They have no feeling of remorse such as is expressed in the words 'The good I have not done, the evil I have done'. The Self alone is perfectly free; nay, the Self is freedom.

20. Leaving out the seeing Self, oneself seeing God is but seeing a mental image. Does he, at least, who sees the Self, see God (How to see) one's ground after one's head is lost? For, the Self is not other than God!

The Self, it has been said in effect, is the solvent of all problems. Where problems arise, there their solution is to be sought for. Problems arise because the ego is mistaken for the Self. They will dissolve only when this fundamental mistake is shaken off. We have seen that the question of fate *versus* free-will defies all attempts at solution so long as we remain at the ego level. The same is the case with regard to the paradoxes of theism.

It is not that theism is to be condemned or that it has no value. Faith in and devotion to God account for a great measure of progress in spirituality. They attenuate the ego and pave the way for its annihilation. The dissipated mind is brought to one point, and its distracting tendency is curbed. The ignorant individual has first to learn that the ego is not all and that there is a power greater than the ego and the world, serving as the ground of them both. He has to extricate himself from the morass of the finite by holding on steadfastly to the Prime Mover of things. So, Advaita recognises the usefulness of theism as a spiritual discipline. But only it would add that one has to go beyond it, for the simple reason that it does not completely destroy finitude. It is said that the mystic attains 'at-onement' with God, but if there is still some difference, the process is not complete. Where there is even the smallest fissure, we cannot have the Whole. As the *Brihadaranyaka* puts it 'He who worships a God thus, "He is different; I am different", does not know; he is a domestic animal to the God.'[1]

The theistic philosophers all the world over have striven to prove the existence of God. But all those arguments have been

---

[1] I, iv, 10.

shown to be fraught with flaws. If God is held to be the first cause, one may legitimately ask why the chain of causes should stop with God. If it is argued that God is the efficient cause, as the potter is in respect of a pot, the critic may well point out that we would then have only a limited God. If God is required as the moral governor of the world of souls, then his role becomes a minor one comparable to that of a paymaster. There are difficulties in conceiving of God as the creator of the universe. There are difficulties in investing him with a personality. So long as it is the ego that seeks to measure truth with its own yardstick, the paradoxes and puzzles relating to God cannot be cleared.

The ego pictures to itself a God in different ways. It attributes to that God all the perfections which it can imagine. Because it is a person, imperfect and finite, it thinks that God is a perfect and infinite person. But any idea of personality necessarily involves imperfection and finitude. All ideas of God formed by the ego contain, therefore, a self-contradiction. This contradiction cannot be removed so long as the ego lasts. It is only when the ego vanishes that the truth dawns — the truth of the non-dual reality which is the Self. We may even call this supreme reality God. Here, terms do not matter but what is important to note is that in the plenary experience there is no distinction at all — not even that of the worshipper and the worshipped.

The Self is the ground of the ego as well as of God. There is no distinction there of the seer, seeing, and the object seen. The distinction is a feature of the lower knowledge, of the pseudo-experience. It is only in the absence of Self-knowledge that there is the empirical usage of seeing. All seeing, including the seeing of God as an *other*, is, therefore, within the sphere of nescience. It is a mental seeing, a seeing by the ego. The forms of God that are thus framed by the mind are images. That these images have their value, we have already said. But they cannot usurp the place of the final truth.

The one who has realized the Self may be said to see the Self. But here, expressions such as realizing and seeing have only a figurative meaning. In Self-realization there is no subject-object distinction. So, even he who sees the Self cannot be said to be seeing God — God in the sense of a personal being set over against the seer. All seeing involving distinction is there, only so long as the ego functions. After the ego has lapsed in Self-knowledge, how can there be any seeing? The supreme truth is that the Self is God, and the Self that is God is not an object of seeing. Indicating the nature of the supreme, the *Kena Upanishad* says:

'That which is not expressed by speech, but that by which speech is expressed — that alone know thou as *Brahman*, and not this which people worship here.

That which is not thought by the mind, but that by which the mind is thought — that alone know thou as *Brahman*, and not this which people worship here.

That which is not seen by the eyes, but that by which the eyes are seen — that alone know thou as *Brahman*, and not this which people worship here.'[1]

yac cakṣuṣa na paśyati
yena cakṣūmṣi paśyati
tad eva brahma tvaṁ viddhi
nedaṁ yad idam upāsate.

21. If it be asked: 'What is the truth of the scriptural texts which speak of oneself seeing the self and seeing God', (we reply) since oneself is one, how can oneself see oneself? If oneself cannot be seen, how can God be seen? Getting absorbed is seeing.

---

[1] *Kena*, i, 5-7. See also the next two verses.

The scriptures, no doubt, speak of seeing the Self and seeing God. But *seeing*, obviously, cannot have its usual meaning here. The Self cannot be seen as an object is seen. It is to teach this truth that, sometimes, the Self is called the seer.

dṛg-dṛśyau dvau padārthau staḥ
paraspara vilakṣaṇau,
dṛg brahma dṛśyaṁ māyeti
sarva-vedānta-ḍiṇḍimaḥ.

'The seer and the seen are two things, mutually exclusive. The seer is *Brahman*; the seen is *maya*. This is the proclamation of all Vedanta.'[1]

It is for the purpose of teaching the aspirant that the Self is described as the seer. The supreme truth, however, is that it is inadequate to apply to the Self even the term 'seer'. It is more appropriate to call it 'sight' or 'knowledge'. So, it is evident that the Self cannot be seen. Because there is nothing but the Self, who is to see whom? In the words of Yajnavalkya, 'By what can the knower be known?'

vijñātāram are kena vijānīyāt?

Since God is identical with the Self, God too cannot be seen. What, then, is the meaning of the scriptural statements about 'seeing'? The meaning is 'realizing the identity' figuratively referred to as 'absorption'. When the ego is destroyed, when, in other words, its illusory nature is realized, all that remains is the Self which is God.

22. Lending light to the mind, (the Lord) shines in the mind. Other than turning the mind within, and lodging it in the Lord, how is it possible to think of the Lord with the mind? Thus should you know.

---

[1] See the *Drig-drisya Viveka*.

Commenting on verse twenty, we quoted a text from the *Kena Upanishad* which says that *Brahman* is not that which is thought by the mind, but that by which the mind is thought. The last verse has made it clear that seeing or experiencing the Self or God is not the ordinary mode in which the object seen is different from the seer. True seeing is realizing one's identity with the Self.

Here the same truth is taught still further. The mind by itself has no power to know. It shines only by borrowed light. The source of all knowledge is the Self which alone is self-luminous. It is the Lord-God who is the Self that lends the light of intelligence to the mind. If the mind is able to reveal objects, it is because of this reflected light. The Self does not stand outside the mind and illumine it; for there is no 'outside' for the non-dual Self. It is the inner ruler of all beings. For the purpose of meditation, scripture declares that the Self resides in the heart. The Self is the ground or basis of the mind.

How, then, to know or think of the Self? The only way is to make the mind turn within and expire in the Self. So long as the mind seeks to maintain its individuality, it cannot know the Self. When it ceases to be, there will be nothing to know. True knowledge is being. The knower of *Brahman* is *Brahman* (*brahmavid brahmaiva bhavati*). The method of knowing is to turn within. Says the *Katha Upanishad* (iv. 1):

parāñci khāni vyatṛṇat svayambhūs
tasmāt parāṅ paśyati nāntarātman,
kaścid dhīraḥ pratyagātmanām aikṣad
āvṛtta-cakṣur amṛtatvam icchan.

'The Lord who is *sui generis* pierced the sense organs to go outward. Therefore one sees outside, and not the inner Self. But a certain wise one saw the inner Self, turning the eye within, desiring immortality.'

23. This body will not say 'I'. In sleep, no one will say 'I am not'. After the 'I' rises, all rises. Enquire with a keen mind whence this 'I' rises.

We have seen that all empirical usage is centred round the ego. It is this ego that is usually referred to as 'I'. But what is this 'I' in truth? What is its nature? Whence does it come? What is its end? In the present verse starts the enquiry into the 'I' which is so vital for understanding Vedanta. Sri Ramana's emphasis on this method is so great that we may rightly describe him as the Prophet of Self-enquiry.

Although the physical body is sometimes denoted by the term 'I', as when one says, 'I am fat' or 'I am lean', it does not take long to distinguish the 'I' from the body. The body itself cannot say 'I', for it is inert. Since even the most ignorant man understands the implication of the expression 'my body' the danger of occasional identification of the 'I' with the body is not grave.

Not so the identification of the 'I' with egoity (*ahankara*). That the 'I'-notion is a superimposition on the physical body, is not difficult to detect. But the subtle superimposition of it on the ego is hard to discard. For, the inquiring mind is the ego, and in order to remove the superimposition, it has to pass a sentence of death on itself. This is by no means easy. The offering of the ego (*atma-nivedana*) in the fire of wisdom is the greatest form of sacrifice.

Yet a little discernment will reveal that the ego is not all. At least a negative evidence we can all have from the experience of deep sleep. One does not say there 'I am not', though the ego had made its exit. The ego does not function in sleep. Still there is the 'I' that witnesses the absence of ego and the objects. If the 'I' were not there one would not recall on waking 'I slept happily; I did not know anything'.

We have, then, two 'I's — the pseudo-'I' which is the ego and the real 'I' which is the Self. The identification of the 'I' with the ego is so strong that we seldom see the ego without its mask. Moreover, all our relative experience turns on the pivot of the ego. With the rise of the ego on waking from sleep, the entire world rises with it. The ego therefore, looks so important and unassailable.

But this is really a fortress made of cards. Once the process of enquiry starts, it will be found to crumble and dissolve. For undertaking this enquiry, one must possess a sharp mind — much sharper than the one required for unravelling the mysteries of matter. It is with the one-pointed intellect that the truth is seen (*drisyate tu agriyaya buddhya*). It is true that even the intellect will have to get resolved before the final wisdom dawns. But up to that point it has to inquire — and inquire relentlessly. Wisdom, surely, is not for the indolent!

What form should the method of enquiry take? The intellect must seek the origin of the ego. In so far as the intellect and the ego are of the same stuff, it amounts to the intellect's search for the ground of itself. What is the basis of the ego which styles itself as 'I'? Whence does it rise?

24. The inert body will not say 'I'. The Existence-Consciousness will not rise. The 'I' of the measure of the body rises in-between. This is (called) the knot of the intelligent and the inert, bondage, the individual soul, the subtle body, egoity, transmigration, mind. Thus should you know.

What is this 'I', the pseudo-'I', which is the hub of all empirical usage, which rising, everything else rises? That the physical body cannot be called 'I' we have already shown. The physical body is inert, unintelligent; and so, it cannot be the sphere of the 'I'-notion. Its appropriate designation is 'this'. The Self which is pure intelligence (*suddha chaitanya*) or existence-consciousness (*sat-chit*) is eternal and has no beginning and end. So, it cannot be said to rise at any time. What, then, is the 'I' that rises? It is a tertiary term, *i.e.*, it is neither the gross body which is inert, nor the Self which is intelligence. Its location, of course, is in the body; its limits are the body. Yet it is distinguished from the body. Figuratively speaking, it may be described as the meeting place of the inert not-Self and the intelligence-Self. It seems to be something very real. But on enquiry it turns out to be void of substance.

What is this strange meeting place? How can the inert and intelligence meet? They are opposed to each other like darkness and light. It ought not to be possible to combine one with the other and to mistake the one for the other. Yet, all our relative experience is built on such a combining and a mistake. This is what is known as *avidya, maya*; also *adhyasa*, superimposition.

By various names is the illicit combination of the inert and intelligence known. It is called the knot of the heart (*hridaya-granthi*) — the knot of the intelligence-spirit and inert matter. This is what constitutes bondage. Other than this there is no individual soul. Individuality is bondage. If this be removed, there is only the non-dual spirit. The individual soul or *jiva* is called *chidabhasa* (reflection of intelligence or pseudo 'I'). What is distinctive of each individual soul is its subtle body (*sukshma-sarira*). It is this which persists till the onset of release. Since the ego is the principal factor in the subtle body, that body may even be called egoity (*ahankara*). It is the egoity that migrates from one birth to another. Hence it is transmigration, the empirical tract of existence. It is also known as mind.

The point that is to be grasped here is this. For a realistic system like the Sankhya, there is a sequence of evolutions, each distinct from the rest and all of them real. Similarly, for a pluralistic realism like the Nyaya-Vaisheshika there is a plurality of realities. But for Advaita there is only one non-dual reality which is Spirit or Self. What seems to be other than this is an appearance. It does not matter by what name it is called.

25. Grasping a form (i.e. body), it rises; grasping a form it stands; grasping a form, it eats and waxes; leaving a form it grasps another form; when sought it takes to flight — this shapeless and ghostly ego! Thus should you know.

The ego appears, but is not real. Its appearance is dependent on a bodily form, gross, subtle or both. We saw earlier that the ego is the basis of all empirical usage, and that it disappears in sleep. In the states of waking and dream it functions — but functions only after seizing a form. When the physical body stands, it thinks 'I stand'. Similarly all other empirical usage is made possible because of this clinging to a body: 'I eat', 'I wax', 'I wane', etc. And, when one body is destroyed, the ego takes on another body. This is what is known as transmigration. Without assuming a body, the ego cannot function. In other words, it has no form of its own. That the body is illusory, we have already shown. When we inquire into the nature of the ego, it turns out to be without substance. It is a veritable ghost which takes shape in fear. To use one of the analogies given by Sri Ramakrishna, the ego is like the onion which is nothing apart from its peels.

26. If the ego is, all else is. If the ego is not, all else is not. The ego, verily, is all. Therefore, the enquiry as to what it is, is but the giving up of all. Thus should you know.

In the previous verse it was stated that the ego appears as dependent on a body. But that does not mean that the body is anterior to the ego or that it is real. The entire world appears only *with* the ego, though not *from* the ego. When on waking the ego rises, the world rises. In dream, the ego sees a fancied world of images. The ego and the world are reciprocally dependent. Without the ego there is no world; and without the world there is no ego. It is in this sense that the ego is all.

The ego is all only so long as one has not begun to inquire into its nature. When the enquiry starts, it is discovered that the ego is nothing. Wherefrom does it rise? From the pure awareness which is the Self. The ego cannot illumine the Self. When the Self, the source of the ego and the world, is realized, the ego along with the world vanishes. True renunciation is the process whereby the ego is made to disappear. It is another name for Self-enquiry.

27. *The state where the 'I' does not rise, is the state where we are 'that'. Without seeking the place where the 'I' does not rise, how is one to attain Self-loss consisting in the non-rise of 'I'? Without attaining that, say, how is one to abide in one's own state where one is 'that'?*

Here by 'I' is meant the ego, and by 'that' *Brahman*. The teaching 'That thou art' does not mean that the ego is *Brahman*, but that the source of the ego, *viz.*, pure awareness which is the Self is *Brahman*.

The realization of our non-difference from *Brahman* comes only when the 'I' dies. That state is called '*turiya*', that which transcends the states of waking, dreaming and sleeping. In waking and dreaming, the ego is manifest, while in sleep it becomes dormant, having resolved itself in nescience. From nescience it emerges again when we wake up or dream. It is only when the illusoriness of these changing states is realized through the wisdom of the non-dual spirit that one attains release. Here, obviously there can be no 'I'.

What is the procedure for quelling the hydra-headed 'I'? Sri Ramana's answer is: Self-enquiry. By seeking the source of the ego, *viz.*, the place whence the ego rises, one puts an end to the ego itself. This is the loss of the lower self, the ego; and this is the greatest gain. What a small price it is that one pays in order to gain the *summum bonum* which is *Brahman*!

When the ultimate reality is gained, what happens? Nothing happens. Even to speak of it as a 'gain' is to use figurative language. It is the *sahaja* state, one's eternal experience that was never truly lost. Only it appeared so. Being 'that' is being oneself, for oneself is 'that'.

28. Just as one would dive to recover something that has fallen into water, even so, one should, with a keen mind, dive into oneself, controlling speech and breath, and find the place whence the swell 'I' rises. Thus should you know.

The technique of Self-enquiry is further explained with the help of an example. If something precious has fallen into water, a diver goes to the bottom and recovers it. But diving requires a certain skill. One cannot be talking while diving; nor can the normal process of breathing go on. The diver controls his speech and breath. He should also have presence of mind. He should have a keen vision and an alert spirit. Similarly, the inquirer into the nature of the Self should have perfect control over his body, sense organs, *prana*, and mind. Disciplines like *asana*, *pranayama*, etc. are not ends in themselves. They are to be looked upon as mere aids to Self-enquiry. In one of his inimitable parables, Sri Ramakrishna says that people who gather for a feast go on talking only till they start eating. When once the process begins, they become quiet. So also, one becomes quiescent automatically when one intensely starts on an enquiry into the nature of the Self. Speech is required up to a certain stage. After that, it becomes a burden and a distraction. Breathing too becomes composed when there is a poise of the mind. Rapid and uneven breathing is symptomatic of mental agitation. *Per contra* regulated and even breathing contributes to the concentration of mind. One may be an adept in *mauna* and *pranayama*: and yet if one does not possess a keen mind, one would not reach the goal. For the vision of the ultimate Self, a sharp intellect is essential. Scripture declares: *drisyate tu agriyaya buddhya* (it is seen by the sharp intellect). It is true that the intellect too has to commit suicide in the final blaze of realization. But all the same it is the door through which one is led to the non-dual spirit. Hence it is that Sri Ramana says that one should have a keen mind. With such a mind one has to track the ego to its source. 'Whence does this blooming, buzzing "I" rise? What is its source?' Thus should one inquire.

29. Without mouthing the word 'I', to seek with the mind turned inward as to whence the 'I' rises is, verily, the path of knowledge. Other than this, the contemplation of the form 'this I am not: that I am' is but an auxiliary; it is not enquiry.

There is no use of repeating 'I', 'I' or any other formula. Such repetition does not take one nearer the truth. The more one withdraws from the externalities the better it will be for discovering the real Self. The enquiry of which Sri Ramana speaks is an inward process. Flitting about a thing and looking at it from the outside is not the way to understand it truly. To repeatedly utter the word 'I' will be such a process in relation to the knowledge of the Self. In order to understand a thing, we must enter into it and reach its core, as it were. The Self is not an object that is external or alien to us. The Self is us. So, the process of enquiry must be directed inward. The instrument, of course, is the purified mind. Rid of its usual distractions and propensities for straying into the non-essentials, the mind must be guided to look within. This method is not to be confused with psychological introspection or subjective meditation. 'Looking within' means discerning the appearances as appearances and getting at their root-reality. The *modus operandi*, as taught by Sri Ramana, is to detect, with ceaseless effort, the source of the 'I' notion. Wherefrom does the 'I' rise? As a result of this enquiry the pseudo-'I' is separated from the real 'I'; the former is realized to be but an appearance of the latter. And what is more, when the real 'I' is realized the pseudo-'I' vanishes. This is the path of *jnana* (knowledge).

Jnana should not be confused with *dhyana* (meditation or contemplation). Meditation is not possible without some illusory identification. The object of identification may be external, or internal. One may meditate, for instance, on the Solar Deity or on some internal principle such as *prana*. The meditation may take the form 'I am not the body, etc. I am *Brahman*.' But what is the 'I' here? It is the ego. The mental identification of the ego with *Brahman* may serve to liberate one from the grosser identifications with such things as the body, etc. With that much, however, the truth is not realized. The ego still lingers, and so long as it does so there is no *Brahman*-realization. *Dhyana* has, no doubt, its own use. It brings the mind to a state of one-pointedness. It prepares the ground for the dawn of wisdom. Wisdom, however, is gained through enquiry, for the one object of enquiry is to make the inquiring mind cease and reveal the non-dual spirit as the sole and whole reality.

30. When the mind, turning inward, inquires 'Who am I?' and reaches the Heart, that which is 'I' sinks crestfallen, and the one reality appears of its own accord as 'I', 'I'. Though it appears thus, the 'I' is not an object; it is the whole. That, verily, is the Self which is real.

The result of Self-enquiry is here stated. When there is persistent enquiry into the nature of 'I', what happens? The pseudo - 'I' vanishes, and the real 'I' shines. The purified mind, as was explained earlier must turn within and direct its light, though borrowed, on itself. The usual way with the mind is to busy itself with the things of the world. Like a maddened monkey drunk with the wine of worldliness, it jumps from one object to another, knowing no rest nor peace which is the end of its quest. What has to be done first is to steady the mind, to make it one-pointed. The method for stilling the mind, as taught by Sri Ramana, is the 'I' enquiry. The question 'Who am I?' of course, rises in the mind. But if it is pursued properly, it will take one beyond the mind. The enquiry, in fact, will lead to the Heart centre which is the seat of reality, the true 'I'. Then, the 'I' alone shines with nothing else besides. There is no subject-object relation there, for the true 'I' is the *whole*. It is *purna*, the *plenum*. Nothing is there before it nor anything after it.

> pūrṇam adaḥ pūrṇam idaṁ
> pūrṇāt pūrṇam udacyate,
> pūrṇasya pūrṇam ādāya
> pūrṇam evāvaśiṣyate.

That is the whole, this is the whole from the whole, the whole arises; taking away the whole from the whole, the whole alone remains.

31. For one who, having destroyed the ego, is awake to the nature of the Self which is bliss, what is there to be accomplished? Other than the Self, he is not aware of anything. How can his state be comprehended?

This verse is in praise of the one who has reached the goal even while tenanting a body — the *jivanmukta*. Enquiry, as we saw, results in the disappearance of the pseudo-'I' and the realization of the true 'I'. The pseudo -'I' is the ego — the subject in all empirical usage. When its nature is inquired into, it 'sinks crestfallen', because it has no title to reality, although it assumes that title till the discovery is made. Self-discovery, therefore, spells the destruction of the ego. In deep sleep, it must be remembered, the ego is not destroyed, but is only resolved in its cause, *viz.*, ignorance. The destruction of the ego takes place with the onset of knowledge. And when there is Self-knowledge, there is release. Release does not await the disintegration of the body which is called death, the reason being that release is one's eternal state. What obscures it, is *avidya* (nescience). When that is removed, the Self's nature as freedom stands self-revealed. This is called *moksha* or release, and *prabodha* or awakening from the slumber of ignorance.

The *mukta* (released soul) is the *buddha* (the awake). He is awake to the nature of the Self which is bliss. Release therefore, is not a condition of emptiness, nor mere absence of sorrow. It is of the nature of unexcellable bliss, the highest value. This is so because *moksha* is the Self. He who gains the Self attains the plenitude of happiness. There is nothing more that he should accomplish, for he has accomplished all that has to be accomplished; he is *krita-kritya*. If there were anything other than the Self, he might want to accomplish it. Since there is nothing besides the Self, what is there to be accomplished by him?

Even to refer to the *mukta* as an individual is not quite correct. He is not an individual among individuals; he is not a 'he'. The difficulty of all speech is that it cannot express what transcends all limitations. In *moksha* there is not even a trace of limitedness. To talk of the 'one that is released' is only a concession to the weakness inherent in language. The plenary

experience that is the Self is all-that-there-is. We that are yet
within the confines of *avidya* may point out to a person and say
'He has attained release; he has become perfect.' But from the
standpoint of the perfect — or rather perfection — there is no
attainment, no becoming. There is no awareness there of
anything other than the Self; the Self is awareness. How can it
be comprehended? For all comprehension involves duality.

*32. While the Scriptures proclaim 'That thou art', without
inquiring as to what one is and abiding (as the Self), to contemplate
'That I am, not this' is because of lack of strength. For, one is always
that.*

For those who are eminently qualified to realize the non-
dual spirit, hearing even once, and understanding the truth of,
the great texts of the Upanishads such as 'That thou art' will be
sufficient. The teaching 'That thou art' occurs in the *Chandogya
Upanishad.* It is imparted to Svetaketu by his father Uddalaka.
Here the teaching starts with the postulation of a reality which
is one without a second. The reality is referred to as *Sat*, existence,
whose Tamil equivalent is *Ulladu.* Uddalaka describes this reality
as that by knowing which everything else becomes known, and
traces the origin of the universe to it. But this origination is not
a real one; it is only apparent. The modifications which constitute
the plurality of the world are mere names. In sleep, and at death,
all these get resolved in the root-reality. But from these states,
the individual returns to the empirical tract of finite existence
because of the persistence of ignorance — ignorance about the
non-dual spirit. He who realizes the truth is liberated from
bondage. What is the truth? It is that there is nothing besides
the one spirit. In that there are no distinctions, even as in the
honey collected by the bees there are no distinctions as 'This is
the honey of this flower; that is the honey of that flower', and as

in the ocean there is no dividing line between the waters of one river and those of another. The spirit is the subtle essence of all things; the whole world has that as its soul; that is the truth; that is the Self. The Self is not somewhere in a remote region, unknown and unrealized; Uddalaka points at his son, Svetaketu, and proclaims 'That thou art'.

Various illustrations are given in order to make the disciple grasp the nature of the non-dual Spirit. Each illustration serves only to indicate an aspect of the truth, and, therefore, should not be pressed too far. The various parts of a tree are held together by its life-force. If the life-force leaves a certain part, that part withers away. Similarly the non-dual reality is the Soul of the universe. Although it is not visible, it is from that invisible Spirit that the universe has arisen, even as from the minute seed the great banyan grows. Reality is omnipresent, even as salt is present everywhere in salt-water. It is not experiencable through the sense organs and the mind; yet it can be realized. The dissolved salt cannot be seen; but it can be tasted. Realizing the Spirit is not like gaining something that is altogether new. It is just returning to our own nature, going back to our home. A man from the Gandhara country was led away blindfolded by a band of robbers. He was left in a lonely and unfamiliar place. At first he did not know what to do. He travelled from village to village asking his way. At last a person that knew the road to Gandhara guided him; and he returned home safely. Just so is the journey to the Spirit. On account of the nescience we have been alienated from the Spirit. Scripture teaches that we are the Spirit. All that remains for us to do is to inquire into the nature of the Spirit and realize it.

Sankara declares that the object of the story of Uddalaka and Svetaketu is to show the oneness of Self. One may be learned in the sacred lore, but if one has not known the truth about the Self, one lives but in vain. The truth is that the Self is extremely subtle, distinctionless, all-pervading, one, undefiled, indivisible, pure consciousness. The Vedanta texts teach this truth either explicitly or implicitly. Following this teaching, says Sri Ramana, one should inquire into the nature of the Self and remain as the Self. There is nothing to be done, here, through the mind, speech, and body. It is only those who lack the strength of knowledge that have to practise contemplation of the form 'That *Brahman* am I, and not this body'. The contemplating ego identifies itself with *Brahman*, and this is not the highest truth. It only serves to lift the contemplator from the lower identifications with the physical body, etc. The highest truth is that the Self alone is. The inquiring mind after leading up to this, must itself lapse. Never was, is, or will be anything other than the Self. One is always the Self.

33. *'I do not know myself', 'I have known myself'* — *to say thus is to invite ridicule. Why? Are there two selves in order to make one's Self the object? The experience of all is that it is one.*

The Self is the only reality. There is nothing other than the Self. So the empirical usage consisting of cognizer, object of cognition, and the means of cognition has no relevance with regard to the Self. The Self cannot be known as an object. Nor is it the content of ignorance. There are not two selves — one which knows and another which is either known or unknown. Such expressions as 'I do not know myself' and 'I have known myself' are incoherent and unintelligible. A sword cannot cut itself. Fire cannot burn itself. It is true that we make use of such expressions. That only shows that being led by the language of *maya*, we land ourselves in 'self-contradiction' 'without our own knowing' — as if the Self can contradict itself and it does not know! Even for explaining the truth one has to employ the language of *maya*.

34. Without realizing, in the quiescent Heart, the reality that is ever the nature of all, and abiding there, to dispute thus: 'It is', 'It is not', 'It has form', 'It has no form', 'It is one, two, neither', is delusion engendered by ignorance.

All verbal discussions about the Self are meaningless. The Self cannot be categorized; it is neither a subject nor a predicate. It neither is nor has anything. We cannot say 'It is', because it does not exist as an entity may be said to exist. To say that 'It is not' is as absurd as to say that 'Virtue is not square'. 'Form' and 'no form', again, are predicates which can be applied only to finite things. We may say, 'Things in space have form; space itself has no form.' As for the category of number, it is entirely out of place. How can the Self be numbered? To say that it is 'one', 'two' or 'neither' is to fall into the trap set by the finite intellect, under the influence of ignorance.

Instead of arguing about the Self and making verbal statements about it, let us be the Self — or to use a slightly better expression — let us realize that we are the Self. Abidance in the Self is *moksha*. This is realized in the Silence of the Heart, which is the symbol of the ultimate reality. When the delusion born of ignorance has been dispelled, there is no room for dispute. The *jnanin* smiles at the debates of the intellectuals. He does not take part in these debates, because he is not a partisan. Advaita is not the doctrine of the partisan. It is the highest experience, and not a theory. Its message — if message it may be called — is 'Cease arguing; BE.'

35. To seek and abide as the (eternally) accomplished existence-reality is (true) accomplishment. All other accomplishments are like the accomplishments that appear in dream. When one wakes up from sleep, are they seen to be real? Will they that are established in the true state and are rid of delusion, be deceived by them? Thus should you know.

Self-abidance, it was stated above, is *moksha*. That is the greatest accomplishment. It is the accomplishment of the eternally accomplished end. A prince grows as a hunter-boy in a family of hunters, not knowing his true parentage. When later he is informed of the truth, he realizes his royal birth. Nothing new comes to him as a result of this knowledge. He is already a prince. Only he is ignorant about the fact. When that ignorance is removed, his true status stands revealed. Similarly, we are the Self. Because of nescience we do not realize our nature as the Self which is existence-reality. We imagine that we are born and we die, that we are confined within the bodies which we call ours, that we are agents and enjoyers, etc. All this is the work of nescience. When through right knowledge nescience is destroyed, we come to our own. It is no new achievement; it is the Self-gain (*atma-labha*), the greatest of all gains.

All other gains are in fact nothing. Sri Ramana compares them to the gains we may have in our dreams. We may strike a huge treasure in our dream and become millionaires, all of a sudden. But of what use is all this treasure in wakeful life? We cannot buy even a meal with the millions acquired in a dream. Similarly, the gains such as wealth and progeny that we seek for and get in our wakeful experience will prove themselves to be myths when we realize the Self. There is not even a hope of immortality through wealth, etc., as Yajnavalkya teaches Maitreyi in the *Brihadaranyaka Upanishad*. When we wake from the slumber of ignorance, the false ends disappear, the unreal vanish. Those that know the truth are not duped by them, for they are no longer under their spell.

36. If we think 'We are the body', to think 'We are not; we are that' is a good aid for us to abide as that. Why should we, for ever, think 'We are that'? Does a man think 'I am a man'? For, we are that.

The abidance as the Self, the supreme Spirit, is, as has already been pointed out, the final goal. It is not an accomplishment of what has not been accomplished. It is the realization of an eternal truth.

Those who have not realized their Self-nature, in other words, those who identify themselves with their body-mind complexes may adopt the method of meditation. Their meditation may take the form: 'We are not the body, etc.; we are the Self'. Such a technique is called *pratipaksha-bhavana*, thinking the contrary. The 'Self-idea' serves the purpose of removing the 'not-Self-idea'. In order that the I-am-the-body conception may be destroyed, the yoga method asks us to cultivate the I-am-the-Self notion. Such practice is certainly useful. But we should remember at the same time that the 'Self-idea' is not the Self, that I-am-the-Self notion is not the supreme Spirit. It is only where all ideas and notions cease that the Self is realized. And, the one who has realized the Self simply is the Self. Such a one has no need to think that he is the Self. Sri Ramana explains this with an example which ought to be familiar to us, humans. A man does not go about saying 'I am a man', 'I am a man'. He need not repeat that as a formula. He simply is a man.

The teaching is that while *dhyana* (meditation) is a useful auxiliary in the path to release, it is not the direct means to release; the direct means is *atma vichara* (Self-enquiry). And in the case of one who has attained release there is no need for meditation at all. He has no mind; how can he meditate? Even to refer to him as a 'he', as an 'individual', is ignorance.

37. That doctrine is not true which says, 'There is duality in practice and non-duality in attainment'. Who else is he but the tenth man, both while anxiously searching for himself and after attaining himself?

It is usual to distinguish between the empirical (*vyava-harika*) standpoint and the standpoint of the absolute truth (*paramarthika*), and to say that the pluralistic world of our ordinary experience is relatively real, though it ceases to be real when the absolute truth comes to be realized. All striving for realization, all practice, is in the world of plurality. In that world there is the distinction between the finite *jiva* and the infinite *Brahman*. It is only when the *jiva* becomes one with *Brahman* by realizing It, that the duality disappears. So, in the world of practice there is duality; in the state of realization there is non-duality.

To argue in the above manner is not sound. There is no double truth. What is called empirical reality is no reality at all. It is not as if the world is real up to the point of Self-realization, and thereafter it disappears. Even when the world appears, it is not real. From the standpoint of the absolute truth, there is no empirical world. The rope does not cease to be rope when it is mistaken for a snake; nor is that snake real even when it appears.

Another illustration is provided by the story of the ten travellers. After crossing a swollen river, the travellers start counting themselves imagining that one of them is lost in the floods. The tenth man is there even when there is a search for him, as he is there when he is discovered.

Non-duality (*Advaita*) is the supreme truth (*paramartha*). It is not something which is made or produced by *sadhana*. Even when there is *sadhana* there is non-duality. Advaita is not what-is-yet-to-be, it ever is.

38. If we are the agents of deeds, we shall have to experience the fruit of deeds. When one knows oneself by inquiring as to who is the agent of deeds, the sense of agency is lost and the threefold karma is removed. And, eternal is the state of release.

That Self-enquiry is the one sure solvent for all the problems of life and thought is the central teaching of Sri Ramana. One of the most knotty of problems is that of *karma*. Even knowledgeable persons go wrong, says the teacher of the *Gita*, in determining what is action and what is non-action. Action does not mean mere movement of the body or functioning of the will. Nor does it mean simply the results of actions that a body-mind complex has to reap or is in the process of reaping. It is only when the Self mistakenly identifies itself with the psycho-physical organism, which is a product of *maya*, that it becomes an agent and an experiencer. Agency and experiencing are superimposed on the Self; they do not belong to it.

Karma, is the sense of action and is of several kinds. There are optional deeds (*kamya-karma*) which one need perform only if one wished for their fruit. He who desires heaven, for instance, is asked to perform sacrifices such as the *jyotishtoma*. There are obligatory duties (*nitya-karma*) which one has to do because they have to be done. The offering of twilight prayers (*sandhya vandana*) is one such duty. The *nitya-karmas* are daily obligations. There are certain other obligations which are occasional (*naimittika-karma*). These too are of the nature of 'ought'. For example, the birth of a son carries with it the obligatory performance of certain rites. While the varieties of *karma* so far mentioned are positive in the sense that they are prescribed for performance, there are others which are negative and therefore prohibited. These are called *pratisiddha-karmas*, such as killing or doing injury to a living being. Actions are also classified into those that are secular (*laukika*) and those that are sacred (*vaidika*). But whatever be the nature of the work, whatever be the category to which it belongs, it springs from *avidya*, and is rooted in it[1].

---

[1] Sankara, *Adhyasa-bhashya: tasmad avidyavad vishayani eva pratykshadini pramanani sastrani ceti.*

Karma, in the sense of 'fruit of action', is of three types. The results that are due to a soul on account of all its actions from beginningless time are called *sanchita* (accumulated karma). Those results for which the soul has taken its present body to experience, constitute its *prarabdha-karma* (i.e., *karma* which has begun to bear fruit). And those results which the soul goes on accumulating and will have to be experienced later in a future birth, are known as *agami-karma* (also *sanchiyamana*). It is usually said that *sanchita-karma* is destroyed through Self-knowledge, that for one who has realized the Self there is no *agami-karma*, but that such a one has to experience in this life the remaining portion of *prarabdha*. The analogy of the rotation of the potter's wheel for a while even after the propelling rod has been removed is given in this connection. Thus it is maintained that the *jivanmukta* has to live in the body till the momentum of *prarabdha* is spent, and that thereafter he becomes a *videha-mukta*.

Such an explanation is not valid from the standpoint of the *mukta*. We have already seen that even the empirical usage of the form, 'He is a *mukta*' is from our point of view, *viz.*, that of the unreleased. There is no individuality whatsoever in *mukti*. Since *avidya* has been removed there is no body either. How, then, can there be *karma*? The Self which is the same as *mukti* or *moksha* has no *karma*; it is not an agent or experiencer. So, when there is release, it necessarily means that all *karma* has been destroyed.

Let us inquire, 'Whose is *karma*? Who is the agent of deeds?' The result of this enquiry will be the realization that there is no agent. In the absence of an agent, how can action be? When the actionless (this does not mean *static*) Self is realized, one is released. And release, as we have noted already, is not a new acquisition. It is the eternal state of the Self.

39. Only so long as there is the thought 'I am bound' will the thoughts of bondage and release last. On seeing the Self through the enquiry as to who the bound one is, and where the Self abides, eternally established and eternally free, the thought of bondage will not stand. And, will the thought of release stand before one?

'Bondage' and 'release' are meaningful only from the relativistic standpoint of the empirical world. Where there is duality, there one may be bound and another released. But the truth is that there is no duality. It is the ego or the mind that is responsible for all such thoughts as 'I am bound', 'I seek release', 'I am to be released', etc. The way to be free from all such thoughts is the enquiry: 'Who is it that is said to be in bondage?' When the inquiring mind ceases, it will be discovered that there was no bondage, that there is no bondage, that there will be no bondage. The Self is eternal freedom. When one abides as the Self, there is no bondage. If there is no thought of bondage, how can the thought of release arise? As Gaudapada declares: there is no destruction or origination; no one bound, nor any engaged in spiritual exercise. There is no one seeking release, nor any released. This is the supreme truth[1].

40. If it be said that the release one may attain is threefold, as with form, without form and with and without form, we say that the release is the destruction of (the triad) 'with form', 'without form' and 'with and without form', and of the distinguishing ego. Thus should you know.

It has already been taught that the distinction between *Jivan-mukti* and *videha-mukti* is an unreal distinction. Some speak also of a threefold *mukti*; (1) with form, (2) without form and (3) with and without form. The first two are the same as *Jivan-mukti* and *videha-*

---

[1] *Karika*, ii, 32. See Gaudapada: *A Study in Early Advaita*, p. 147.

mukti, respectively. The moment one realizes the Self, one is released even while tenanting the body. The body continues for a while because of the remnant of *prarabdha* which has to be exhausted. This is release with form. The release without form happens when the body falls at the expiry of *prarabdha*. The third variety 'with and without form' is the release which is enjoyed by the *adhikarika muktas*, whose mission it is to save the world. After shedding the physical body, they live in the subtle body for the welfare of humanity. They are also called the *chira-jivins* (those with long life). These three types of *mukti* are but mere names. They have a meaning only on the side of the world, and not from the standpoint of the supreme truth. True release consists in freedom from even the notion that there are three kinds of release. As the Vedantins say, the very idea of release too is bondage (*moksha-sankalpa-matro-bandhah*). It is only so long as the ego lasts that there is ideation. When the ego is destroyed, there is no talk or thought of even release. The means to realize egolessness is Self-enquiry. Therefore, know the SELF. This is the message of Maharshi Ramana.

PART II

SUPPLEMENT

(*Anubandham*)

INVOCATION

Wherein stays all the universe, whereof is all this, wherefrom all this universe rises, wherefore is all this, whereby all this universe rises, which all this becomes — that alone is the existence-reality, the truth; that form let us place in the heart!

This invocation is in the form of contemplation of the root-reality, Brahman. As it is difficult to realize the unconditioned reality, it is first taught as the ground of the universe. Brahman is the *total* cause of the world. It does not *change into* the world. The world is only an *appearance* of Brahman. Brahman in itself is pure existence-reality.

It is noteworthy that Sri Ramana employs here the various case-endings with reference to the world-ground, in order to indicate that it is the all-sufficient cause, and also to lead us from the conditioned to the unconditioned reality. There are eight cases on the whole; nominative, accusative, instrumental, dative, ablative, genitive, locative and vocative. In the present verse, Sri Ramana begins with the locative case, and then employs the others in an ascending order. There is no explicit use of the vocative. The accusative appears in the expression '*that form*'. In 'which all this becomes', 'which' is in the nominative case.

There are quite a few verses in Sanskrit which make use of all the case-endings. The following is from Kulasekhara's *Mukunda-mala*.

krṣṇo rakṣatu no jagat-traya-guruḥ
krṣṇaṁ namasyāmy ahaṁ
krṣṇenāmaraśatravo vinihatāḥ
krṣṇāya tasyai namaḥ
krṣṇād eva samutthitaṁ jagad idaṁ
krṣṇasya dāsosmy ahaṁ
krṣṇe tiṣṭhati sarvam etad akhilaṁ
he krṣṇa samrakṣa mām.

(May Krishna, preceptor of the worlds, protect us! To Krishna do I bow. By Krishna were the enemies of the gods destroyed. For that Krishna this obeisance. From Krishna alone has arisen the world. Of Krishna, I am a slave. In Krishna stays all this world entire. O Krishna, protect me!) In Sivajnana-munivar's gloss on *Nannul,* there is a Tamil verse illustrating all the case-endings. But here, each case-ending relates to a different world.

THE TEXT

1. By association with the good (the real, the true) attachment (to the world) will go; when attachment goes, the modification of the mind (with its cause, maya) will be destroyed; those who are free from mental modification are those who are one with the changeless (reality); they are those who have attained release while living (in the body). Cherish their company!

For a spiritual aspirant, association with those that are spiritually awakened is of inestimable value. The ordinary mind is greatly influenced by the company it keeps. Environment counts in the shaping of one's nature. A *sadhaka* must see to the propriety of his environment. There cannot be a better environment than that provided by the good and the true.

The most fortunate is he who lives in the presence of a *jivanmukta*. It is not possible to demonstrate discursively as to who is a *jivanmukta*. Such a one is more to be intuitively felt than to be reasoned about. *Jivan-mukti* is itself a mystery. One who has attained it leads others also to it. The function of a *jivanmukta* is to serve as the exemplar of the perfect life on earth.

The teaching Sri Ramana imparts to us in the present verse is the same as what Acharya Sankara says in a well-known stanza:

sat sangatve nis-sangatvam
nis-sangatve nirmohatvam,
nirmohatve niścalatatvam
niścalatatve jīvan-muktiḥ.

'When there is association with the good, there is non-attachment; when there is non-attachment, there is freedom from delusion; when there is freedom from delusion, there is the status of changelessness; where there is changelessness, there is release-in-life.'

2. *That supreme place, which is attained through the discriminating enquiry of the mind which has come into relation with the good (jivanmuktas), is not attained through one who merely teaches about it, or through perpending the meaning of texts, or through meritorious deeds, or through any other means.*

This is in praise of the *jivanmukta*. Devotion to him purifies the mind and plunges it into Self-enquiry. A *sadhaka* who enjoys the presence of a *jivanmukta* requires no other means. Listening to expositions of scriptural texts, performing good deeds, etc., cannot compare with the privilege of living in the proximity of a *jivanmukta*. It is not that they have no value; they are helpful. But the greatest help one can get is from a *jivanmukta*. The *mukta* need not even talk. His very presence has the potency to save the devotee from his delusion.

3. *If one lives in the company of the good, what for are all these rules-of-life? When the superior cool southern breeze blows, where is the need, say, for a fan?*

If one has gained the grace of a *guru* who is a *jivanmukta*, then one need strive for acquiring nothing else as the means to wisdom that liberates. The object of all disciplines is the purification and concentration of the mind. Association with a *jivanmukta* accomplishes even more than this. If there is the southern breeze blowing, of what use is a fan? When there is an all-engulfing flood, who would go in search of a lake?

4. *Heat is removed by the cool moon, poverty by the good kalpaka tree, and sin by the Ganges. But all the three, heat, etc., will get removed by the incomparable benign look of the good.*

Physical heat and mental worry may, for a time, be allayed by the cool rays of the full moon. The earthly wants may be removed with the help of the mythical wish-fulfilling tree. The Ganges water may wash away one's sins. But these are powerless to destroy *avidya* which is their cause. It is only the gracious look of the *jivanmukta* that can do away with nescience. Hence there is nothing that can compare with it.

5. *The sacred bathing places which are in the form of water and the images of gods made of stone and clay are not at all equal to those great ones. Lo! they may purify (a person) after countless days, but know (that there is immediate purification) when the good ones see with their eyes.*

The fruit of bathing in sacred rivers, etc., and of worshipping images of the gods is unseen (*adrista*). Such pious acts may bring in *punya* which affords happiness in a hereafter or a future good birth. But the gracious look of a guru removes the cause of all worry immediately and without any residue.

6. *'Who is God?' 'He who knows the mind.' 'My mind is known by me who am spirit.' 'Therefore, you are God'; and also because scripture declares: 'One only is God'.*

Here the enquiry into the truth begins. To the question 'Who is God?', the reply is 'He who knows everything including the so-called knowing mind is God'. It is the witness-Self that knows the mind. It is that which shines without the aid of any other light. It is that which does not depend on anything else. It is that which cannot be divided, and is one. It is that which is indicated by the notion 'I'. That is God.

7. *'What serves as the light for you?' 'For me, the light during the day is the sun, and during the night the lamp.' 'What is the light that sees these lights?' 'The eye.' 'What is the light that understands it?' 'The Mind.' 'What is the mind that knows the mind?' 'The "I".' 'The light of all lights are you.' Thus taught by the teacher, (the disciple realized :) 'That, verily, I am'.*

The figure of light is employed in the Upanishads to teach the nature of the Self as consciousness. External lights are helpful in revealing the objective world. But even thus, they alone will not do. There must be the appropriate sense-organ to make use of the lights. The sense-organ, in its turn, must be illumined by the mind; and the mind by the Self.

It is only in the state of waking that the external lights like the sun, the moon, lamps, etc., are available. In dream, even in the absence of these, there is experience. The mind creates its own lights as well as the objects. In sleep, even the mind ceases to function. Yet, there is experience which is the

Self. Hence, the Self alone is self-luminous. It is the sole, never-failing light.

8. In the middle of the cave of the heart, the one Brahman alone shines as the Self, as 'I' 'I'. Resort to the heart; sink by meditating on the Self. Or, by the mind which sinks along with the breath, resort to the heart alone. You will thus become stationed in the Self.

Brahman is the heart of everything; it is the Self of all. It shines in all sentient beings as 'I'. One has to reach it by discrimination. Meditation on the Self implies enquiry into its nature. The control of breath is one of the aids. Breath-control facilitates the quiescence of the mind. When the mental functions cease through Self-enquiry, the self-luminous heart-centre which is *Brahman* is realized.

9. The awareness which is of the nature of the undefiled and unmoving 'I' in the heart-lotus — that awareness which is 'I' grants liberation by removing egoity. Know thus.

When through Self-enquiry the true 'I' is realized, the pseudo-'I' which is egoity disappears. Such realization is what is called liberation. The true 'I' is of the nature of pure awareness that is ever present. It is the constant and unfailing light. For the purpose of facilitating concentration, its seat is said to be the lotus of the heart.

10. The body is inert like a pot, since it does not shine, as 'I', and since in its absence in sleep we always are, 'I' am not the body. Who is the maker of 'I'-ness? Where is He? In the heart-cave of those who have realized, the omnipresent Arunachala Siva shines of His own accord as the 'He-I-am' consciousness.

The three key expressions used here are: *naham deham* (I am not the body), *koham* (Who am I?) and *soham* (I am

He). The first realization is that the body is not the Self. Two reasons are given: (1) the body is non-conscious, like a pot; and (2) in the state of sleep the body is not experienced and yet there is awareness. If the body is not the Self, what is the Self? Through persistent enquiry, one realizes that God is the Self (He am I).

11. He alone is born who, after inquiring 'Where was "I" born?' is born in the root-Brahman; he is ever born; he is the supreme sage; he will ever be new. Know thus.

True birth is spiritual birth. He who realizes the Self is the twice-born. But, his is not a birth in time. It does not become old. It cannot be dated. The sage is not an individual. Sagehood is the plenary experience gained through Self-enquiry. It is *Brahman*-experience, and so is designated *Brahman*-birth.

12. Leave off thinking the despicable body as the Self. Know the Self that is the uninterrupted happiness. Attempting to know the Self while cherishing the ephemeral body, is like using a crocodile as a float to cross a river.

Non-attachment is an essential requisite for Self-enquiry. Of all attachments, the attachment to one's body is the most difficult to conquer. Hence the aspirant must cultivate an attitude of non-attachment to his own body. But this will become possible only when he is convinced that the Self is the supreme seat of happiness. Vedanta does not advocate a life of mere negation. Attachment to body, etc., is bad because it stifles the soul and brings in sorrow. One is asked to be non-attached to them because that is the way to realize the Self which is unexcellable and perennial bliss. One cannot serve two masters — the body and the Self. Nor can one realize the Self by trusting the body.

The body is not something which is to be cherished as if it were stable and abiding. 'I-am-the-body-consciousness' is ignorance. This can never serve as the means to Self-realization.

13. Charity, penance, sacrifice, merit, psychic control, devotion, heaven, substance, peace, truth, grace, silence, the supreme state, the deathless death, knowledge, renunciation, release, happiness — know that these are but the severance of the notion that the body is the Self.

The various spiritual disciplines, the different conceptions of the goal, the several modes of expressing the nature of the reality — all these are included in the plenary experience which is freedom from 'I-am-the-body-consciousness'. Destruction of ignorance and release are the same. And, release is the Self.

14. The enquiry, to whom are the fruit of deeds, non-devotion, disunion and ignorance, is itself karma, bhakti, yoga and jnana. When thus inquired, the 'I' goes, and the abidance as the Self wherein these never are, is verily the truth.

He who imagines that the fruit of deeds is his and that he is affected thereby, is asked to pursue the path of unselfish work (*karma*); he who believes that he is away from God is asked to attach himself to God, to be devoted to Him (*bhakti*); he whose mind is dissipated and directed towards different ends is asked to practise psychic control in order to attain one-pointedness (*yoga*); he who is aware of the ignorance that is the cause of bondage is asked to seek knowledge (*jnana*). The result of all these disciplines one gets by Self-enquiry. When one inquires into the truth of the Self, one discovers that there is neither fruit nor deed, neither separation nor union, and that ignorance too is not in reality. It is the ego that is in bondage and that strives for release. When through Self-enquiry the 'I' disappears, all-that-is is the Self. No duality is there; no relation of end and means; no bondage, no striving, no release.

15. The conduct of the lunatics who say 'We shall gain all the supernormal powers', not realizing that they themselves are moved by sakti (divine power), is like the story of the lame man who said, 'If I am helped to stand, where will these enemies be?'

Attachment to the body and its normal functions is itself despicable. The body appears and operates in and by *maya*. There are some *yogins* who seek to glorify and reinforce this deception by consciously aspiring for gaining supernormal powers. Supernormal prowess is a delusion and a snare. It only increases the ego and makes it cripple all the more. Already there is the handicap of body-consciousness. If the desire for *siddhis* (supernormal powers) be added to it, then the condition of one becomes extremely pitiable. Of course, such a *yogin* may bluster and brag. But all this will be of no avail; and with this he will not be able to assail and vanquish the enemy, which is ignorance.

16. As the quiescence of the mind is the eternally established release, say, how can those whose mind is attached to the supernormal powers, which cannot result without the activity of the mind, achieve the happiness of release which destroys all modifications of the mind?

Those who are after supernormal powers go through a path which cannot lead to release. Release is obtained only when all the desires of the mind cease, when the mind itself gets destroyed. The desire for supernormal powers only reinforces bondage. Those who seek them enter deeper into the dark regions of *avidya* (nescience). There is no release for them.

17. While for bearing the burden of the earth there is the Lord, to imagine that the pseudo-self bears it, is a mockery like the (imagined) bearing of the temple-tower by the image (that is sculptured therein). Whose fault is it, if a man who travels in a cart carrying a heavy load carries his luggage on his head, without placing it in the cart?

Those who imagine that on them rest the fortunes of the world are deluded. It is God that is the ground and ordainer of all things. The world is His manifestation. Saving it is His function. For individuals to imagine that the course of things depends upon them, that they are the arbiters of history, is sheer delusion. The world does not wait upon any single individual. No one, however great he may be, is indispensable for the maintenance of the world. If any good is done at all in any way by any individual, it is done not by that individual's inherent power, but by the might of God. The individual is himself an illusory projection of *maya*. How can he sustain the world of *maya*? Two examples are given: (1) The image that adorns a temple-tower might have its hands and disposition sculptured as if it were holding the tower; but in reality the stay of the tower does not depend on it. (2) A traveller who is in a train may carry his luggage on his head, out of ignorance. But the truth is that it is the train that carries both him and his luggage. If he knew this, he would disburden himself of the luggage and travel free.

This does not, however, mean that an individual does not have the obligation to serve his fellow beings. Work has to be done; but it is the spirit of worship that must pervade it. Egoistic social service will do nobody any good. It is selfless service that is divine service. Let not the social worker imagine that he is going to transform the world, that upon him depends the destiny of mankind. Let his service spring out of humility and devotion. So long as the pluralistic outlook governs him, let him behave as a servant of God.

18-19. Between the two breasts, below the chest and above the abdomen, there are six things of varied hues. Of these, the one resembling the lily bud that remains within, two digits to the right, is the heart.

It faces downward. In it there is a small orifice. Therein resides a dense darkness, along with desires, etc. All the great *nadis* have that as their support. It is the seat of vitality, mind and the light (of intelligence).

Here is a description of the spiritual — and not the physical — heart. A physical location is assigned to it to facilitate meditation. The heart is the seat of the Self. It is also the centre where all the faculties of individuality meet, and their cause, *viz.*, ignorance, resides.

20. The Lord who shines in the cave of the heart-lotus, his home, is, verily, praised as Guhesa (Lord of the Cave). If by the strength of practice (abhyasa) the continued thought 'I am He' (soham), that is 'I am Guhesa' becomes firm, even as the 'I' notion that is firm in your body, and if you remain as that Divinity, then the ignorance which is of the form, 'I am the body' whose nature is to perish will be dispelled even as darkness before the rising sun.

It was stated above that the heart is the seat of both the Self and ignorance. There is a knot, as it were, of the Self and the not-Self. If this knot is to be cut, ignorance must be destroyed. Here a method whereby this could be effected is taught. The notion 'I am the body' is to be countered by the meditation of the form 'I am the Self'. When the notion of 'Self' becomes firm, it will uproot the contrary notion of identity with the body. Even as the darkness of the night is dispelled by the rising sun at dawn, the metaphysical ignorance which is responsible for bondage and suffering gets destroyed through Self-knowledge.

21. 'That huge mirror in which all this (universe) appears as an image, that which is said to be the heart of all the souls in this universe — what is that, please explain'. To Rama who thus enquired, the sage Vasishta explains: 'When one thinks about it, (it will be seen that) twofold is the heart of all souls in this universe.'

In our note to verses eighteen and nineteen, we said that these verses give a description of the spiritual, and not the physical, heart. As the physical body itself is an illusory appearance, to locate the heart in a part thereof is also an act of superimposition. To explain this the teaching of the *Yoga-Vasishta* is here recalled.

22. '*What is to be accepted and what is to be rejected — listen to the characteristics of these two. The organic member called the heart which is situated at a particular place inside the chest of the measurable body is what is to be rejected. The heart which is of the form of the one consciousness is what is to be accepted. Thus you should know. It is both within and without. It is not that which is in the inner space.*'

The physical heart is the pseudo-heart. The real heart is the Self which is of the nature of pure consciousness. The real heart is everywhere, and cannot be confined to any particular place. 'Inside' and 'outside' have no meaning with reference to it; for it is not space-bound. The spaceless Infinite which is the heart supreme is the only reality.

23. '*That alone is the heart supreme. In it all this resides. It is the mirror of all things. It is the abode of all wealth. Therefore, it is said, the (one) consciousness of all souls is alone the heart. It is not a part of the physical body which is inert like a piece of stone and which is perishable.*'

As the Self is the sole reality, there is nothing apart from it. It is the ground of all things; on it are all things illusorily superimposed, as images in mirror. It is the supreme goal of all life; it is the highest value. Hence it is said to be the heart of all beings. The physical heart, surely, cannot answer to the above description.

*24. 'Therefore, by the discipline which consists in merging the
ego in that pure heart, of the nature of consciousness, the quiescence
of the vital air will of itself result, as also the destruction of the
residual impressions of the mind.'*

The method by which the real heart is to be realized is
Self-enquiry. When by this method the ego suffers self-loss, the
Self alone remains. The *vasanas* (residual impressions) of the
mind vanish, and there is no need, then, for breath-control.

*25. 'That consciousness which is devoid of all conditioning
adjuncts — that Siva am I: thus there should always be the
uninterrupted meditation, whereby you should remove all
attachments from the mind.'*

The purpose of meditation is to make the mind still and to
empty it of all attachments. The meditation of the form 'I am
Siva (God)' is for countermanding the deep-rooted notion of the
form 'I am the body'. When I-am-the-body notion disappears,
the Self is realized to be the sole reality, the unconditioned
consciousness which is the heart of all beings.

*26. 'Having inquired into all the various states (waking,
dreaming, and deep sleep), and always holding firmly at heart
that which is the supreme goal, free from delusion, play in the world,
O hero! You have realized that which is within, as the truth of all
kinds of appearances. Therefore, without ever losing that sight, play
in the world as you like, O hero!'*

Here is Sage Vasishtha's instruction to Rama: Enquiry into
the three states of experience is the means to realize the truth
that the Self is the sole reality. When this realization becomes
constant, the delusion of plurality gets destroyed. Then one may
play one's part in the world, without being affected thereby.

What is important to note is that such a one never loses sight of
the real, which is the ground of all appearances.

*27. 'With apparent emotions such as pleasure, with apparent
agitations such as hatred, and with apparent endeavour in initiating
activity, but without attachment, play in the world, O hero! Having
obtained release from all sorts of bondage, having gained equanimity
in all situations, performing actions outwardly according to your
part, play in the world, O hero!'*

A spiritual aspirant acts his part in the world, as any other.
But his actions, and the emotions which are behind them are
only apparent. He seems as if elated or depressed, but is not
really so. Similarly, he appears to plan and execute projects. He
seems to do all that a worldly man does. But he knows the
unreality of it all. As in a play, he merely acts out his part; and
he is not affected by what happens. This is because of his state
of desirelessness and equanimity.

*28. He who is steady in the truth of knowledge is the knower
of the Self. Through knowledge he has destroyed the sense impressions.
He indeed is Agni, who is knowledge. He is Indra, with knowledge
as his weapon (vajra). He is the Time of time. He is the hero who
has destroyed death. Thus do you proclaim!*

This is in praise of the one who has realized the Self.
Knowledge is the means to Self-realization. In the case of one
who has gained Self-realization through knowledge, the sense-
functionings and their impressions have no effect. In fact, for
the one who is liberated in life (*jivanmukta*) there are no sense-
organs, no body, and no mind; for him there is no world of
duality. His knowledge is compared to fire (*Agni*) which burns
all dross, and to the weapon (*vajra*) of Indra with which the

demon Vritra was killed. He who has realized the Self is not conditioned by time. He is the Time of time or Death of death (Siva). He is the real hero (*dhira*), who has no fear at all, even of death, for there is no 'other' who or which can cause fear.

29. For those who have seen the truth, illumination, intelligence and strength will of their own accord increase, even as when the spring comes all excellences such as beauty, etc., adorn the trees of this earth.

In the *jnani* one finds the culmination of culture. He need not cultivate any excellences; they come to him automatically. Even as the spring brings fullness of life and beauty to nature, so does Self-realization to the soul.

30. Even as those whose mind is far away listen to a tale, the mind whose impressions have been destroyed does not (really) function, although it may (appear to) function. (On the contrary) the mind which is full of those impressions functions although it may not (appear to) function; even as those, though motionless here, climb up a hill in a dream and fall into a pit.

What is action and what is non-action, it is difficult to determine from the 'outside' point of view. The body may be active, while the mind is at rest, and *vice versa*. Properly speaking, activity arises from the mind and its impressions (*vasanas*). At the base of activity is the notion 'I act'. Where this notion is absent, there is no activity. Where this notion is present, even though there is no overt activity, there is activity. This is illustrated by two examples. One may appear to be listening to a story; but if his mind is away at the time he is not, in fact, listening. The dreamer's body is stretched motionless in a bed; but in his dream he is intensely active.

31. Just as for a man who is asleep in a cart, the going of that cart, its stopping, and its being left alone are (the same), even so are, for the true knower who is asleep in the cart of the gross body, activity, concentration and sleep.

Here is the parable of the cart. The gross body is the cart. The senses are the horses. And the sense-objects are the roads. For a *yogi* who has not 'realized', there are three states; the state when he is externally active, that in which he is composed and collected (*samadhi*), and sleep. These are compared respectively to the cart in motion, the cart in station, and the cart from which the horses have been unyoked. To the person who has realized the Self, there are not these states, just as for a man who is asleep in a cart the three conditions thereof are not real. For the *jivanmukta* there is not the mind-body complex; the changing conditions of the latter do not, therefore, affect him.

32. Beyond the reach of those who go through waking, dream and sleep, there is what is known as waking-sleep. There is that transcendent experience (turiya) alone; and there are not the apparent three. Hence that is the transcendent turiya. Know thus.

Although the *jivanmukta* has been compared to the sleeper in the cart, his state is not that of sleep. The three states of waking, dream and sleep belong to those who are in bondage. The pure experience which is that of the *mukta* is beyond them, and is called the *turiya* (the fourth) and even *turiyatita*. Although this experience is referred to as the *fourth* (*turiya*), it is not really a fourth *in addition* to the three empirical states. On the contrary, it is the underlying basis of those three states; it also transcends them. So it is called *turiyatita*. Some scholars seek to distinguish *turiya* from *turiyatita* or *turiya-turiya*. But there is no need for such a distinction. The transcendent state is the plenary experience. It is described as *waking-sleep* because one who has this experience is *awake* in the Self and *asleep* in the world. In the language of the *Gita*, where the wise are awake, the worldly are asleep, and *vice versa*.

33. *The accumulated fruit of works (sanchita) and the works yet to come (agami) do not belong to the wise one; works that have begun to fructify (prarabdha), however, remain — thus to say is only in reply to the query put by others (the ignorant). Realize that just as after the husband is gone no unwidowed wife would remain, even so when the doer is gone, the threefold works would also (be gone).*

There is a problem connected with the *jivanmukta's* continuance in the body. If the body is the result of *karma* and *avidya*, and if for the *mukta* there is no *avidya*, there should be no *karma* also. How then, could the continuance of the body be accounted for? The reply that is usually given is this: *karma* is threefold — *sanchita* (all the accumulated works), *agami* (future works), and *prarabdha* (that portion of the past works which is responsible for the present body). In the case of the *jivanmukta*, the *sanchita* has been burnt in the fire of knowledge, and there is no *agami* because the sense of agency has been destroyed. The *prarabdha*, however, has to be enjoyed, and as long as this lasts the body has to continue. This is explained by means of various examples. Imagine a bowman, who has a quiver of arrows on his back, has let go an arrow from his bow, and is about to shoot another. He may throw away the quiver of arrows (which is like the *sanchita*) and decide not to shoot hereafter (*agami*). But as regards the arrow that has left his hands (*prarabdha*), it must do its work, and there is no escaping from it. The continuance of the *jivanmukta's* body is also compared to the rotation of the potter's wheel even after the propelling rod is removed. The wheel will continue to rotate till the momentum is spent, and then stop of its own accord. Although the *jivanmukta* has to enjoy his *prarabdha*, this does not affect him and does not give rise to fresh *karma*. *Prarabdha* in his case is like fried grain which could be eaten but does not sprout.

The line of answer sketched above is from the standpoint of the ignorant. It is to the ignorant that the *jivanmukta* appears to tenant a body. From the standpoint of the *mukta* himself there is no body. In fact, even to refer to 'him' as an 'individual' is due to our ignorance. Therefore, the so-called distinction between *jivan-mukti* (release in embodiment) and *videha-mukti* (release without body) is without any difference. In *mukti* there is no body at all. The answer given above may be all right in the Sankhya system where embodiment is real, where the one really becomes the many. For Advaita, however, embodiment is illusory along with the world-process. So, the doctrine that there is *prarabdha* for the *jivanmukta* is a *hereditas damnosa* from the Sankhya.

The true solution for the problem is that for the *jivanmukta* there is not even *prarabdha*. Sri Ramana offers an illustration. When a husband dies, all his wives without exception become widows. Similarly, when the sense of agency is gone, there is no *karma* at all. It may be contended that *prarabdha* requires only an enjoyer, and not an agent. But there is no point in this contention. It is the ego that acts and enjoys; and for the *jivanmukta* there is no ego at all.

34. For those who are of little wit there is a single family consisting of children, wife and others; but inside the mind of those who have wide learning there is not one family but several consisting of many books, serving as obstacles to yoga. You should know this.

It is shown here that learning can become a burden. The arts and the sciences have their own use. They may instruct the intellect and add to the advantages of living. But they do not show the way to liberation. Even the reading of Vedantic texts will become burdensome if it is not for the higher purpose of spiritual realization. It is the thought complexes that bind the soul. They constitute *samsara*. These complexes in the case of the learned man are formidable. He gets caught in the complicated web of his own theories. Pitiable indeed is his plight.

35. What is the use of knowing the letters, if those who know them do not inquire as to where they were born and thus seek to wipe out the writ of Fate? They are like the gramophone. What else are they say, O Arunachala?

Narada confessed to Sanatkumara that he knew only the letters and not the spirit. And so he was sorrow-stricken. Those who are but masters of letters are in the present verse compared to the gramophone. The voice-machine can only reproduce mechanically what has been recorded. It does not know the meaning of what it reproduces. Similarly, those who are merely learned in the books do not profit much. They should rather inquire about the 'I' which thinks it is learned. Whence is this 'I' born? What is its nature? It is this 'I'-enquiry that will lead to the conquest of fate — to release from *samsara.*

36. Better than those who are learned but not subdued, are those who are not learned but saved, for they are saved from the grip of pride: saved from the disease caused by the many roving thoughts and words: saved from wandering all over the country in quest of wealth: thus know that it is not from one (ill) that they are saved.

It is to be noted that the pride of learning is worse than the uninstructed pride. The ordinary pride can be easily got rid of, but not the learned pride.

The learning that is not motivated by the highest purpose of spiritual illumination has many disadvantages: it increases one's pride, makes the mind restless and distracted and drives one to hunt for wealth and more wealth. The man without learning is at least free from these burdens.

Sri Ramana's condemnation of mere learning does not mean that he is opposed to education. This condemnation is to be understood as *arthavada*. The sciences and arts may widen the mental horizon and make life easy. But there is a higher goal set for man, namely, Self-realization.

His learning, therefore, should not tend to obscure this goal. He should not carry his books, like the donkey that plods on with a load of sandalwood on its back.

37. Even though all the world is but dust and all the scriptures are in the palm of their hand, those who are in the control of the wicked prostitute of flattery find it difficult, alas, to free themselves from the slavery.

Some may be learned in the Vedanta and, as a result of the learning, may regard the world as illusory and valueless. But even they are liable to fall a prey to flattery. The subtle pride of learning and of being superior is very hard to remove. So long as there is egoity, even the learned and ascetics are beguiled by the sense of being distinct.

38. Other than the Self who is there? What if anyone says anything about the Self? What if one extols or denounces oneself? Without differentiating as oneself and others, and without swerving from one's natural state, one should abide ever as the Self.

It is only the *jivanmukta* that stays unaffected by flattery and abuse. There is no 'other' to him. How can another praise or blame him? It is just like praising or blaming oneself. He is one who remains steady in wisdom (*sthitaprajna*). Wisdom is the experience of non-duality. Where there is no 'other', extolling and denouncing become impossible.

39. Keep the truth of non-duality ever at heart; never should you translate non-duality into action. O Son, although non-duality with all the three worlds may be all right, it is not proper with the preceptor. Thus should you know.

There is the danger of understanding the meaning of Advaita wrongly. When it is said 'All is One', 'You are that', etc., one may superficially interpret these statements to mean that A, B, C, D, etc., are one. Obviously, if there are A, B, C and D as distinct entities, they cannot be one. Advaita does not teach that these distinctions are one, nor that they should be reduced to one. In the Advaita experience there is no plurality at all. And so, it is not the express sense of the Advaita statements that should be taken as what they teach, but their implied meaning.

The story is told of a student who attempted to practise non-duality as against an elephant. His teacher taught him that 'all is *Brahman*'. As he was walking along a road he saw an elephant coming. The mahaut who was seated on the elephant asked the student to get out of the elephant's way. But the student would not listen. Why should he leave the middle of the road, he thought; after all he was *Brahman*, and the elephant too was *Brahman*; and how could *Brahman* harm *Brahman*? As he was musing in this manner, the elephant caught hold of him with its trunk and threw him aside. With his body mangled, he went to his teacher and complained that the teaching he had received did not work. The teacher remarked: 'When *Brahman* in the form of the mahaut asked you to move away, why did you not listen to him?'

There can be no action without duality. Behaviour is possible only when there is the cognition of duality. While cognizing duality, to argue that there is no difference between good and evil, high and low, preceptor and pupil, is not to know the meaning of Advaita. The pupil, so long as he is a pupil and has the body-consciousness, should show the highest reverence to his master.

The original Sanskrit stanza of which the present verse is a Tamil rendering is as follows:

bhādvādvaitaṁ sadā kuryāt kriyādvaitaṁ na karhicit
advaitaṁ triṣu lokeṣu nādvaitaṁ guruṇā saha.

40. *The quintessence of the established conclusion of all the Vedanta texts I shall declare in truth: when the ego dies, and the 'I' becomes that (Brahman), that 'I' which is of the nature of consciousness alone remains. Thus should you know.*

Sri Ramana concludes the supplement with a statement of the quintessence of Vedanta; what we refer to in ignorance as 'I' is not the Self but the ego. When through enquiry the pseudo - 'I' disappears, the real 'I' is realized.

That is Self-realization or non-dual experience. The existence that is reality is non-dual. It is the plenary experience, the absolute Self.

PART III

REFLECTIONS

I. THE SAGE OF ARUNACHALA

TIRUVANNAMALAI (Arunachala in Sanskrit) is one of the most sacred places of pilgrimage for the Hindus, as God is worshipped there in the form of Light. Once in a year the holy beacon is lit on the top of the hill; and thousands of people go thither to see the light and adore it. But all through the year, the place has now become an international port of call for spirituality, because Maharshi Ramana lived there for over half a century shedding the flame of God-realization.

As a young lad in his teens, he went to Arunachala, and since then he made it his life-abode. The very name Arunachala served as an imperious call from the Divine, and he simply obeyed the call. The exalted state of egolessness came to him; and once it comes, it never goes. Strictly speaking, it is not one state among other states of experience; it does not come nor occur in a given moment of time. It is the eternal status (*sahaja-sthiti*). Because of *avidya* (nescience) one does not recognise it. And when *avidya* is made to disappear, the self-luminous nature of the spirit shines. This is what is called *moksha* in Vedanta. It is not an after-death experience. The continuance of the body is not inconsistent with release. It is only identification of the Self with the ego, etc., that is an obstacle to realization. When that obstacle has been removed, one becomes a *jivanmukta*, free while living. We hear of many such great souls in our scriptures. But in the Maharshi we had a contemporary *jivanmukta*, a living commentary on the most sublime texts of the Vedanta. Many a

statement of the scriptures, like the one in the *Bhagavad Gita*
about seeing inaction in action and action in inaction, will
remain obscure and unintelligible, unless one comes into contact
with sages like the Maharshi. Apparently, Sri Ramana seemed
to take interest in things that happened around him. He
recognised people and sometimes talked to them. Even creatures
belonging to the sub-human species claimed his attention. He
used to lend a helping hand even in the kitchen by dressing
vegetables for cooking. But all these modes of action were
performed without the least attachment to them. In truth, they
were no actions at all, since they were void of egoity. The core of
activity had been removed; only the shell remained; and that
too for us, the onlookers. Nothing seemed to affect this Rock of
Ages. He stood as a witness to all phenomena. The distinctions
of high and low had no meaning for him. The stranger and
foreigner who visited him felt absolutely disarmed and free even
at the first sight. One may be foreign to another or look strange;
but how can one be alien to oneself? The Maharshi who had
crossed the boundaries of individuality naturally and effortlessly
felt — if we may use such a poor word — *one* with all. Like the
pandit (the wise one) of the *Gita*, he looked upon all as the
same — the high-born and the lowly of birth, the cow and the
elephant, the dog and the dog-eater — these classifications may
have meaning for us who are caught in the network of difference.
To him who had *seen* the non-dual *Brahman* which is *sama*, the
same, there was no plurality, no difference.

It was a delightful and unique experience to sit in the
presence of the Maharshi, and look in the full glare of his beatific
eyes. One might go to him with a medley of doubts and
questions. But very often it happened that these upsurgings of
the mind died down and were burnt to ashes as one sat before

the Sage. One had a foretaste of that pristine state, of which the Upanishad speaks, when the knot of the heart is cut and all the doubts are dispelled. One stepped back and watched how the turbulent mental stream quietened down and received an undisturbed reflection of the self-luminous Spirit. What one might succeed in attaining after a prolonged course of Yogic discipline, one got with perfect ease and effortlessly in the proximity of the Maharshi. True, this experience might not stay for long. One might get back to the world and wallow again in the dirt of worldliness. But still, the impress of spirituality that had been gained was never lost. Seldom was one, the depths of whose soul had been stirred by the sublime look of the Sage, without the desire to go again to him and receive fresh intimations of the eternal. People sometimes went to him in the hope that by his *darshan* (look) their earthly wants would be fulfilled. But very soon they discovered their own foolishness in asking for fleeting pleasures, when the imperishable *bliss* awaited them. Instead of getting dissatisfied that their cravings went unfulfilled, they would feel thankful that they had been saved from a delusion and a snare. Nachiketas of the *Katha Upanishad* was offered by Yama all the pleasures of all the worlds in lieu of Self-knowledge for which he had asked; but the true son of spirituality that the boy was, he refused to be tempted into accepting the pleasant in the place of the good. The Maharshi who to us was the personification of the supreme Good transmuted our lower passions and desires into *moksha-kama*, an intense longing for release.

Some went to the Maharshi with a curiosity to get from him a cure-all for the world's ills. They used to ask him what solution he had for the problems of poverty, illiteracy, disease, war, etc. Social reform was their religion; a re-ordering of society was what they sought after. They framed their questions in different ways. What message had the Maharshi to give to the social reformer? Was it not the duty of every enlightened citizen to strive for bettering the lot of his fellowmen? When misery and squalor were abroad, how could anyone who had a feeling heart keep quiet without exerting himself in doing his bit for world-welfare? The invariable answer that the Sage gave to all those who put such questions was: 'Have you reformed yourself first?' Very often it happens that so-called social service is a self-gratification of the ego. In much of what passes for altruism, there is a core of egoism. Such service blesses neither the server nor the served. The former's pride increases, and the latter's demoralisation is made complete. It is only such service as that which contributes to the reduction of the ego that is the harbinger of good. And the influence of the ego cannot be lessened unless one knows, however remotely, that the ego is not the Self, that it is only the pseudo-self, responsible for all the evil and misery in the world, and that the final and lasting felicity could be realized only when the root-cause of the ego, *viz.*, ignorance, is dispelled. And so, unless one seeks to know the true Self, one cannot do real service to society. Reform must begin with oneself. He who is on the path renders service to fellow-beings so that his ego may be cleansed and become attenuated and ready to be discarded. And he who has realized the End and has become a *jivanmukta* performs work — or more correctly appears to us to perform work — in order that the world may be saved (*loka-sangraha*). So Self-enquiry is the basis of true service; and Self-knowledge is its culmination.

The Sage of Arunachala had no new message for humanity. What he taught through silence more than through words was the ageless gospel of the Vedanta. Sankara cites in his *Sutra-*

bhashya text from the *Smriti* in which it is stated that when approached by Badhva for instruction, Sage Baskali kept quiet, and, on being questioned again and again, said 'We have declared the truth already, but you have not understood: the Self is peaceful, quiet (*upasanta*).' The Maharshi's teaching was exactly the same as that of the Upanishadic sage. He seldom spoke. It is in the stillness of silence that the depths of the spirit are reached. Words and thoughts cannot lead us far enough. Even the words of scripture help us only up to a point; and there they must stop. It is said of young Dakshinamurti that he taught his elderly disciples in the language of silence. It is true that only a few can understand what is taught in silence. And so, sometimes the Maharshi used to talk. But he warned his interlocutors at the same time, that both questions and answers belonged to the realm of *avidya* (nescience), though the latter did serve as signposts towards the light of wisdom. Doubts would assail the mind so long as the mind lasted. It was only when the eternal state of mindlessness (*amanibhava*) was realized that all doubts of the mind and questionings of the heart would roll away like mist before the rising sun.

The Maharshi's teachings may be stated aphoristically thus: *Seek to know the Self, and the knowledge will make you free.* The *Chandogya* records the story of Narada, master of many sciences and arts, going to Sanatkumara and confessing that he was sorrow-stricken, though he was very learned. He knew that all his learning would be of no avail and that Self-knowledge alone could save him. So he approached Sanatkumara with the request 'Help me across the ocean of sorrow', and received from him the wisdom about the great, the true Self. The supreme commandment of scripture is 'Know the Self' (*atmanam viddhi*). The Maharshi has said over and over again that *atma-vichara* is the one sure and

inescapable path to liberation or release. Other *sadhanas* may help
in this process more or less remotely. It is *jnana* alone that is the
direct means to *moksha*.

This is essentially the view of Advaita Vedanta. And the reason
for it, is that *moksha* is the eternal nature of the Self and not
something which is to be newly acquired or accomplished. No
operation, either of the body or of the mind, can bring about release.
The ever free status of the Self is not recognised because of the
ignorance which veils the true and projects the untrue. When this
ignorance is removed, one realizes one's eternal nature as the non-
dual, unconditioned Self. That which effects the removal of
ignorance is wisdom. And what paves the way for wisdom is *atma-
vichara*.

The enquiry 'Who am I?' is not to be regarded as a mental
effort to understand the mind's nature. Its main purpose is 'to focus
the entire mind at its source'. The source of the psychosis 'I' is the
Self. What one does in Self-enquiry is to run against the mental current
instead of running along with it, and finally transcend the sphere of
mental modifications. It is comparatively easy for us to disentangle
ourselves from wrong identification with the physical body and
material objects. But the identification with the ego is hard to get
over. As the *Panchapadika*, a commentary on Sankara's *Sutra-bhashya*
says, 'The conceit "I" is the first superimposition on the Self.' The
outer layers of ignorance may fall away easily. The last one, however,
is difficult to tear. The best way to remove it is to track it down to its
source. When there is awareness of the source which is the Self, the
ego vanishes. And when the 'I' has been crossed out through *jnana*,
there is no more bondage and consequent sorrow.

The cessation or non-cessation of the body has nothing to do
with release. The body may continue to exist and the world may
continue to appear, as in the case of the Maharshi. That makes no

difference at all to the Self that has been realized. As Sankara says, 'There is no need to dispute, whether the knower of *Brahman* bears the body for some time or not. How can another object to one's own experience, realized in the heart, of *Brahman*-knowledge as well as continuance of the body?' In truth there is neither the body nor the world for him; there is only the Self, the eternal Existence (*sat*), the self-luminous Intelligence (*chit*), the unexcellable Bliss (*ananda*). Such an experience is not entirely foreign to us. We have it in sleep, where we are conscious neither of the external world of things nor of the inner world of dreams. But that experience lies under the cover of ignorance. So it is that we come back to the fantasies of dream and the world of waking. Non-return to duality is possible only when nescience has been removed. To make this possible is the object of Vedanta. To inspire even the least of us with hope, and help us out of the slough of despond, is the purpose of such illustrious exemplars as the Maharshi.

Sri Ramana's example is unique because he did not first read and then experience. Experience came to him first; and only later he found corroborative evidence in the scriptural texts. To an unbelieving world which is impatient and wants to burn its sacred books, Sri Ramana has this message to offer, viz., *that the real book of life is within, and that if we but turn to it and consult its pages, it will open up undreamt-of vistas leading to limitless felicity and bliss.*

II. DAKSHINAMURTI, SANKARA AND RAMANA

In the *Sankaravijaya* of Madhavacharya there is a verse which says that the image of Siva in the form of Sankaracharya goes about in the world, having emerged from the seat under the banyan tree giving up the attitude of silence, in order to save all beings that are fallen into the deep pit of ignorance and

are being scorched in the flames of transmigration, by imparting
to them the teaching about the Self.

ajñānāntargahana-patitān ātmavidyopadeśais
trātuṁ lokān bhavadavaśikhātāpapāpacyamānān,
muktvā maunaṁ vaṭaviṭapino mūlato niṣpatantī
śambhor mūrtiś carati bhuvane śankarācāryarūpā. iv: 60

Siva, as Dakshinamurti, is the world-teacher, who sitting
underneath the banyan tree, teaches the supreme truth through
silence. He is pictured as a youth dispelling the doubts of aged
disciples without the aid of words. But all cannot comprehend
the language of silence; nor is it given to all to go to the banyan
tree where the Lord is seated. So, the need arose for Sankara-
Incarnation. Sankara came as the *jagad-guru* (world-teacher);
only, here, instead of the *jagat* (world) going to the *guru* (teacher),
we have the *guru* coming to the *jagat*. In the short span of thirty-
two years that constituted Sankara's earthly life, a revolution
was effected in the then known India through almost incessant
travel and unsparing exertion on the part of the Master. It seemed
as though the Lord rose from his seat under the banyan tree
leaving off His silence, and moved and mingled with the
multitudes in order to enlighten and save them. In the place of
the unmoving (*achara*) Dakshinamurti, we have Sankara moving
(*chara*); and in the place of silence (*mouna*), we have auspicious
speech (*sankari-vak*). This change or transformation was required
to meet the challenge of the time in which the Sankara-
Incarnation took place.

Our age, the era of machinery and speed, has its own
problems. One finds almost everyone moving without purpose.
A good volume of talking goes on every minute, much of it
without sense. In such an atmosphere of speed and sound it is

no wonder that silence and stasis are often mistaken for spirituality. This age demands on the part of a world-teacher neither absolute silence nor much speech, neither total stasis nor constant movement. We had such a teacher in Bhagavan Sri Ramana who was both *achara* (unmoving) and *chara* (moving), who taught both through silence and speech. Leaving Madurai as a boy of seventeen, Sri Ramana went to Tiruvannamalai and never left that sacred place thereafter. His movement was confined to the environs of Arunachala. To his devotees he was the moving Arunachala. For many years after his arrival at Tiruvannamalai, he did not speak; people used to refer to him as the *mauna-swami* (silent ascetic). But his silence was not part of any discipline. He found no use for words. When at long last he was discovered, and a few ardent seekers of Truth approached him for instruction, he did speak. In short, Sri Ramana played the roles of Dakshinamurti and Sankara to suit the exigencies of our age. If Sankara may be described as the later Dakshinamurti, Sri Ramana, it seems to me, may rightly be regarded as the later Sankara (*apara-Sankara*). In the *Guruparampara-stotra* composed by Kavya Kantha Ganapathi Muni, the following lines occur:

dakśiṇāmūrti-sārambhāṁ
śaṅkarācārya-madhyamāṁ
ramaṇācārya-paryantāṁ
vande guru-paramparām.

'Obeisance to the line of preceptors with Dakshinamurti in the beginning, Sankara in the middle and Ramana in the end!'

It is significant that Sri Ramana has rendered into beautiful Tamil verse Sankara's *Hymn to Dakshinamurti*, adding his own invocation to Sankara at the beginning.

mannuma munivarar santi mannave
tenmukha murtiyayt tigalndu monaman
tannilai tigalttiyit tutiyir ranmayan
connavac cankaran runnumennule.

'That Sankara, who appeared as Dakshinamurti to grant peace to the great ascetics (Sanaka, etc.), who revealed his real state of silence, and who has expressed the nature of the Self in this hymn, abides in me.'

Iswara (God), *Guru* (Preceptor) and *Atman* (the Self) are but different names for one and the same reality. Dakshinamurti, the south-facing Deity, Sankara, the peripatetic Teacher of humanity, and Ramana the Sage of Self-enquiry are expressions of the same principle. In the introductory verse to his verse-rendering of Sankara's *Atmabodha*, Sri Ramana declares his identity with Sankara thus:

anmavin bodhamarulum asanan cankaranav
vanmavuk kanniyanavano-vanmavay
ennahatteyirundinru tamil colvanum
annavananri marrar.

'Is the teacher Sankara, who grants the knowledge of the Self, other than the Self? Remaining in my heart as the Self, he who utters the Tamil today — who is he other than that one himself?'

III. RAMANA EXPERIENCE

He alone can be said to have known Sri Ramana, that has had the Ramana experience. And, he that has had that experience will not know him, remaining outside of him. To know Ramana is to be Ramana. To be Ramana is to have the plenary experience of non-duality. In the absence of that experience, we can only seek to know him by 'description.' This itself is not without its value. Through knowledge by description we may succeed in gaining knowledge by identity. It is a *sadhana* (discipline) of supreme potency, therefore, to be constantly aware of one's acquaintance with Sri Ramana.

To meet a sage and be acquainted with him is not an ordinary occurrence. It must be the result of a good stock of merit. I consider myself extremely fortunate, therefore, to have had the privilege of meeting the Master, when I was barely eighteen. As I recall those three days I spent basking in the sunshine of Sri Ramana's Glorious Presence, I have no word to express the benefit I derived from that experience. To sit before him was itself a deep spiritual education. To look at him was to have one's mind stilled. To fall within the sphere of his beatific vision was to be inwardly elevated.

The most remarkable feature about the Master that struck even a casual visitor was his beaming face. There was no need, in his case, to frame the head in a halo. Such an enchantingly bright face with a soothing look and never-failing smile, one can never forget having seen it even once. The brightness remained undiminished till the very end, even when the Master's body bore the cross of the last illness. A few days before the *mahasamadhi* when I went into the room where he lay and touched his feet with my head and quickly saw the condition in which his body was, I was on the point of shedding tears. But immediately I saw his face and he made kind inquiries in his usual inimitable way, all sorrow left without a trace, and there was Eternity looking on and speaking.

Even when I first saw the Master, his head had begun to nod. The shaking head seemed to me to be saying '*neti*', '*neti*' (not this, not this). And, all on a sudden the nodding would stop, the vision of the Master would become fixed, and the spirit of silence would envelop everyone present. In the stillness of the Heart, one would realize that the 'Self is peaceful quiet' (*santo' yam atma*). Many of those who came with long lists of questions used to depart in silence after sitting for a while in the Master's presence. When some did put questions to him, they received the replies they deserved. It was evident that many could not even frame their questions properly. In such cases Sri Ramana himself would help in the framing of questions. When he chose to answer questions or instruct through words, it was a sight for the gods to see. Each sentence was like a text from the Upanishad, so full of meaning that it required calm silent pondering over in order to be understood. Sri Ramana's answers never remained on the surface. He would go straight to the root of a question and exhibit to the wondering questioner the implications of his own question which he could not even have dreamt of. Often the Master would make a questioner resolve his own doubts. But each time, the supreme Lord would gently guide the seeker to the state of inner silence where all doubts get dissolved and all questionings cease.

There was no occasion when I experienced the manifestation of supernormal powers sometimes attributed to the Master. He seemed to me to be perfectly *normal*. It is we that were *abnormal* by contrast. We have our tensions and mental tangles. As for the Master there was no ruffle, not even the least agitation. The storms of the world never reached him. Sitting or reclining on the couch in the Ashram Hall, he appeared to be 'the still point of a turning world.' There was not the least suggestion of his appearing to be other than normal. His mode of referring to his person as 'I' and not as 'this' was itself significant. He did not want to appear distinct from the rest of us with regard to empirical usage. Yet, there was no doubt about the fact that there was not the least *adhyasa* present in him. His last illness quite clearly demonstrated this. What complete and utter detachment from the body he manifested in order to teach the world that the body is not the Self!

Having been a student of the *Gita* from childhood, I saw in the Bhagavan a vivid and living commentary on that great Scripture. When I was asked to address a meeting held in the local High School during one of my early visits to Tiruvannamalai, this is what I said: 'If anyone wants to understand the inner meaning of the *Gita*, he must come to our town and meet the Maharshi.' In 1948-49, when I was in the United States lecturing on Vedanta, many friends asked me if there was anyone living in India answering to the truth of the Vedanta. My reply invariably used to be 'Ramana'. On my return to India when I went to the Ashram, I had the unique opportunity of giving an account of my American visit to the devotees gathered at the evening worship in the presence of the Master. I repeated to the gathering what exactly I had told American friends; and it was a pleasant surprise to find one or two Americans there whom I had known earlier.

The critics of Advaita usually say that the Advaitin is an austere intellectual in whom the wells of feeling have all dried up. Those who have seen the Master will know how unfounded such a criticism is. Sri Ramana was ever brimming with the milk of divine kindness. Even members of the subhuman species had their share of the unbounded love of the Master. He was a consummate artist in life. Anything that he touched became orderly and pleasant. Sweet and firm was his person even as the sacred Arunachala is. Why should I say 'was'? Even now he is and ever will be the light that never fades, the sweetness that never surfeits, to those who desire wisdom and eternity.

IV. SALUTATIONS TO SRI RAMANA

Those who have had the privilege of meeting Bhagavan
Sri Ramana even once will ever remember the reposeful form,
the benign face and the bewitching eyes. As a lad of seventeen,
he heard the Divine Call and went from the City of the Fish-
eyed Mother (Madurai-Meenakshi) to the Hill of the Holy
Beacon (Arunachala) where the World-Father presides, only to
be transported into the realm of transcendent Bliss, where all
forms vanish and distinctions disappear. From 1896 when Sri
Ramana arrived in Arunachala (Tiruvannamalai) to 1950 when
he shoved off his physical frame, he did not move from the
precincts of the Sacred Hill, but remained there even as an open
book from which anyone that had the requisite inclination could
learn the way to everlasting life. Countless people in their
thousands went to him, some in quest of worldly success and
some in search of the eternal Self. While the Master pitied the
plight of the former, he knew that they too would eventually
join the ranks of the latter. He shed his lustre on all alike; his
eyes showered their blessings on high and low without any
difference. Many a spiritual aspirant found solace in his presence
and illumination in his silence. He taught through words too;
but those words were so designed as to lead the hearer to the
region of silence which is the Self.

Sri Ramana did not found any new school of thought or
cult. He taught the ageless truth of Vedanta which is not sectarian
but universal. Even to call that truth Advaita (non-duality) is
only a concession to the inherent limitations of language. The
Master blazoned forth anew the path of Self-enquiry through
which everyone can attain Advaita-experience. None was too
low for it, and none too great. Everyone can take to it, no matter

what his cult, creed or caste is. Even a sceptic or agnostic, an atheist or anti-theist may follow it and come to good. As Sri Ramana's presence was accessible to all without let or hindrance, so was his teaching meant for the good of the entire world.

As the night drew in on Friday the 14th of April, 1950, Bhagavan Sri Ramana chose to leave his body. But he has not gone anywhere. There is no departure for a *jivanmukta*. And the Master's Mission can end only with universal salvation. Of course, he knows what instruments to choose and in which ways to fulfil his task. Those of us who have had the rare good fortune of association with his embodied form have a sacred duty to ourselves, which is to meditate on him and his teachings, and share with others the precious legacy we have received from him.

APPENDIX I

ULLADU NARPADU

(Transliterated Text in Roman)

Mangalam

1. ulladala dullavunar vullado vullaporu-
   lullalara vullatte yullada — lullamenu
   mullaporu lullaleva nullatte yullapadi
   yullade yulla lunar.

2. maranabhaya mikkulavam makkalara naha
   maranabhava milla mahesan — sarana me
   sarvartan carvodutan charvurrar savennan
   charvaro sava davar.

Nul

1. namulahan kandala nanavan cattiyula
   vormudalai yoppa lorutalaiye — namavuruc
   chittiramum parppanun cerpadamu maroliyu
   mattanaiyun tana mavan.

2. mummudaai yemmadamu murkollu mormudale
   mummudalay nirkumenru mummudalu — mummudale
   yennalahan kara mirukkumatte yankettut
   tannilaiyi nirra ralai.

3. ulakumeypoyt torra mulakariva manren
   rulakusukha manren ruraitte — nulakuvittut
   tannaiyorn donrirandu tanarru nanarra
   vannilaiyel larkkumop pam.

4. uruvanta nayi nulahupara marra
   muruvanta nanre luvarri — nuruvattaik
   kannurudal yavanevan kannalar katciyundo
   kannaduta nantamilak kan.

5. udalpancha kosha vuruvadana laindu
   mudalennun colli lodungu — mudalanri
   yundo vulaha mudalvit tulakattaik
   kanda rularo kalaru.

6. ulakaim pulanga luruveran ravvaim
   pulanaim porikkup pulana-mulakaimana
   monram porivaya lorndiduta lanmanattai
   yanriyula kundo varai.

7. ulakarivu monra yudittodungu menu
   mulakarivu tanna loliru — mulakarivu
   tonrimarai darkidanayt tonrimarai yadolirum
   punrama mahde porul.

8. eppeyarit tevvuruvi lettinumar peruruvi
   lapporulaik kanvaliya dayinumam — meypporuli
   nunmaiyirran unmaiyinai yorndodungi yonrudale
   yunmaiyir kana lunar.

9. irattaikan muppudika lenrumonru parri
   yiruppava mavvonre denru — karuttinut
   kandar kalalumavai kandava reyunmai
   kandar kalangare kan.

10. ariyamai vittarivin ramarivu vittav
    variyamai yinraku manda — varivu
    mariya maiyumarkken rammudalan tannai
    yariyu marive yarivu.

11. arivurun tannai yariya dayalai
    yariva dariyamai yanri — yarivo
    varivayar kadarat tannai yariya
    varivari yamai yarum.

12. arivari yamaiyu marradari vame
    yariyuma dunmaiyari vaga — daridar
    karivittar kanniyamin rayavirva darra
    narivagum palan rari.

13. nanaman tanemey nanava nanaman-
    nanamam poyyaman nanamume — nanaman
    tannaiyanri yinranika dampalavum poymeyyam
    ponnaiyanri yundo pukal.

14. tanmaiyunden munnilaipa darkkaika damulavan
    tanmaiyi nunmaiyait tanayndu — tanmaiyarin
    munnilaipa darkkai mudivurron rayolirun
    tanmaiye tannilaimai tan.

15. nikalvinaip parri yirappedirvu nirpa
    nikalka lavaiyu nikalve — nikalvonre
    yinrunmai tera tirappedirvu teravuna
    lonrinri yenna vunal.

16. namanri naledu nadedu nadunga
    namudambe nanattu nampaduva — namudambo
    naminran renrumonru nadingan gengumonra
    namundu nanadi nam.

17. udanane tannai yunarark kunarndark
    kudalalave nanra nunarark — kudalulle
    tannunarndark kellaiyarat tanoliru naniduve
    yinnavartam bhedamena ven.

18. ulakunmai yaku munarvillark kullark
    kulakalava munmai yunarark — kulakinuk
    kadara mayuruvar rarumunarn darunmai
    yidakum bhedamivark ken.

19. vidhimati mula viveka milarkke
    vidhimati vellum vivadam — vidhimatikat
    kormudalan tannai yunarnda ravaitanantar
    sarvaro pinnumavai sarru.

20. kanun tanaivittut tankadavu laikkanal
    kanu manomayaman katchitanaik — kanumavan
    rankadavul kandanan tanmudalait tanmudalpoyt-
    tankadavu lanriyila tal.

21. tannaittan kana ralaivan ranaikkana
    lennumpan nulunmai yennaiyenin — rannaittan
    kanalevan ranonrar kanavona derralaivar-
    kanaleva nunadal kan.

22. matikkoli tantam matikku loliru
    matiyinai yulle madakkip — patiyir
    padittiduta lanrip patiyai matiyan
    matittiduta lennan mati.

23. nanenrid deha navila durakkattu
    naninren raru navilvadilai — ranon
    relundapi nella meluminda nanen
    gelumenru nunmatiya len.

24. jadavudana nennadu sacchit tudiya-
    dudalalava nanon rudikku — midaiyilidu
    ciccadaggi rantibandhan jivannutpa meyyahandai
    yiccamu saramana men.

25. urupparri yunda murupparri nirku
    muruppari yundumuka vongu — muruvit-
    turupparrun tedina lottam pidikku
    muruvarra peyahandai yor.

26. ahandaiyun dayi nanaittumun dagu
    mahandaiyin relin ranaittu — mahandaiye
    yavuma madalal yadidenru nadale
    yovudal yavumena vor.

27. nanudiya dullanilai namaduva yullanilai
    nanudikkun tanamadai nadama — nanudiyat
    tannilappaic charvadevan charamar ranaduvan
    tannilaiyi nirpadevan charru.

28. elumbu mahandai yelumidattai niril
    vilunda porulkana vendi — mulukudalpor
    kurndamati yarpeccu muccadakkik kondulle
    yalndariya vendu mari.

29. nanenru vaya naviladul lalmanatta
    nanenren gundumena nadudale — nananeri
    yamanri yariduna namaduven runnarunai
    yamaduvi charama ma.

30. nana renamanamun nadiyula nannave
    nana mavanralai nanamura — nananat
    tonrumonru tanagat tonrinuna nanruporul
    punramadu tanam porul.

31. tannai yalittelunda tanmaya nandaruk-
    kennai yuladon riyarrudarkut — tannaiyala
    danniya monru mariya ravarnilaimai
    yinnaden runna levan.

32. aduniyen rammaraika larttidavun tannai
    yeduvenru tanrern dira a — daduna
    niduvanren rennalura ninmaiyina lenru
    maduveta nayamarva dal.

33. ennai yariyena nennai yarindena
    nenna nagaippuk kidanagu — mennai
    tanaividaya makkaviru tanundo vonra
    yanaivaranu bhutiyunmai yal.

34. enru mevarkku maiyalba yulaporulai
    yonru mulattu lunarndunilai — ninrida
    dundin ruruvaruven ronriran danrenre
    sandaiyidan mayaic calakku.

35. chittama yulporulait terndiruttal siddhipira
    siddhiyelan coppanamar siddhigale — niddiraivit-
    tornda lavaimeyyo vunmainilai ninrupoymmai
    tirndar tiyanguvaro ter.

36. namudalen renninala namaduven rennumadu
    namaduva nirpadarku narrunaiye — yamenru
    namaduven rennuvade nanmanida nenrenumo
    namaduva nirkumada nal.

37. sadhakatti leduvidan saddhiyatti ladduvida
    moduginra vadamadu munmaiyala — vadaravayt
    tanredun kalun tanaiyadainda kalattun
    tanrasama nanriyar tan.

38. vinaimudana mayin vilaipayan ruyppom
    vinaimudala renru vinavit — tanaiyariyak
    kartat tuvampoyk karumamun runkalalu
    nittama mutti nilai.

39. baddhana nennumatte bandhamutti chintanaikal
    baddhana renrutannaip parkkungar — chittamay
    nittamuttan ranirka nirkader bandhachintai
    muttichintai munnirku mo.

40. uruva maruva muruvaruva munra
    murumutti yenni luraippa — nuruva
    maruva muruvaruva mayu mahantai
    yuruvalitan mutti yunar.

APPENDIX II

ULLADU NARPADU — ANUBANDHAM

(Transliterated Text in Roman)

MANGALAM

Viruttam

edankanne nilaiyagi yirindidumiv
vulagamela medana della
medaninriv vanaittulagu melumomar rivaiyavu
medanpo rutta
medanaliv vaiyamela melundidumiv vellamu
meduve yagu
madutane yulaporulan cattiyama maccorupa
mahattil vaippam.

NUL

Venba

1. sattinak kattinar charbagalun charbagalac
   chittattin sarbu chidaiyume — chittacchar
   barra ralaiviladi larrarji vanmutti
   perra ravarinakkam pen.

2. saduravu saravulan chartelivi charatta
   ledupara mampadamin geydumo — vodumadu
   bodhakana nurporular punniyattar pinnumoru
   sadhakattar charavona dal.

3. sadhukka lavar sahavaSa nannina
   ledukka minniyama mellamu — metakka
   tandenran marudan tanvisha vevisiri
   kondenna kariyani kuru.

4. tapantan chandiranar rainiyanar karpakattar
papandan gangaiyar parume — tapamuda
limmunru megu minaiyilla sadhukka
damma darisanattar ran.

5. kammayaman tirthangal kanmannan deyvanga
lammahattuk katkinaiye yagava — mammavavai
yennina larruymai yeyvippa sadhukkal
kanninar kandidave kan.

6. devana rarmanan teruva nenmana
maviya menna Iaripadume — devani
yagume yagaiya larkkun curudiya
lekanam devane yenru.

Viruttam

7. oliyunak kedupaga linanenak kirulvilak
koliyuna roliyedu kanaduna rolyedu
volimati matiyuna roliyedu vaduvaha
molitani loliyuni yenaguru vahamade.

Veru

8. idayaman guhaiyi nappa nekamam biramma matra
maduvaha mahama nere yavirndidu manma vaga
vidayame sarvay tannai yenniya laladuvayu
vadanuda nalma natta lanmavi nitta navay.

Venba

9. ahakkama latte yamala vacala
vahamuruva magu marive — dahattai
yagarriduva dalav vahama marive
yahavi dalippa dan.

Viruttam

10. dehan gatanigar cadamidar kahamenun tigalvilada
    nahan cadalami ruyilini rinamuru namadiyalar
    kohan karaneva nulanunarn dularulag guhaiyulle
    soham puranava runagiri sivavibhu suyamolirvan.

Venba

11. piranda devanran biramamu latte
    pirandadeva nanenru penip — piranda
    navane piranda navanudamu nisa
    navanavana vanrinamu nadu.

12. illivudalya nenna ligandiduga venru
    molivilin pandannai yorga — valiyu
    mudalomba lodutanai yoravunal yaru
    kadakkak karappunaikon darru.

13. danan tavamvelvi danmamyo gambhatti
    vanam porulsanti vaymaiyarul — monanilai
    sagamar savarivu sarturavu vidinban
    dehanma bhavamara rer.

14. vinaiyum vibhatti viyogaman nana
    minaiyavaiyark kenrayn didale — vinaibhatti
    yogamunar vayndidana ninriyavai yenrumira
    nagamana leyunmai yam.

15. sattiyinar ramiyangun tanmanyuna radakila
    siddhikanan cervamenac cettikkum — pittarkut
    tennai yeluppividi nemmattit tevvarenac
    connamuda vankathaiyin codu.

16. chittattin santiyade chittama muttiyenir
    chittattin seygaiyinric chiddhiyac — chiddhikalir
    chittancer varennan chittak kalakkantir
    muttisukhan toyavar moli.

17. bhubharan tangavirai poliyuyir tangaladu
    gopuran tangiyuruk koranikan — maparangol
    vandiselu vansumaiyai vandivai yadutalai
    kondunali kondadevar kodu.

Viruttam

18. irumulai nadumar badivayi ridanme
    lirumup porulula nirampala vivarru
    loruporu lampala rumbena vulle
    yiruviral valatte yiruppadu midayam.

19. adanmukha migalula dahamula sirutulai
    yadanila sadiyo damarndula diruntama
    madanaiya sirittula vakilama nadika
    laduvali manadoli yavarrina diruppidam.

Veru

20. idayamalarg guhaiyahama yilagiraiye
    guhesanena vettap patto
    nidamanaiya guhesanya nenunsoham
    bhavanaita ninnu dambir
    ridamuruna nenundidampo labbhiyasa
    balattalat tevay nirkir
    sidaiyudana nenumaviddai senkatiro
    nedirirulpor chidaiyu manre.

21. epperunkan nadiyinkan nivaiyavu
    nilalaga vedire tonru
    mippirapan cattuyirkat kellamav
    vidayamena vishaippa dedo
    seppudiyen revinavu miramanukku
    vasittamuni seppukinra
    nippuviyi nuyirkkella midayamiru
    vidhamagu mennun kale.

22. kolattakka duntallat takkaduma
    mivvirandin kuru kela
    yalattarka mudambinmar bahattoridat
    tidayamena vamainda vangan
    talattakka dorariva karavida
    yankollat takka damen
    rulattutkol lahdullum puramumula
    dulveliyi lulla danram.

23. aduvemuk kiyavidaya madankanniv
    vakilamume yamarndi rukku
    maduvadi yepporutku mellaccel
    vangatku maduve yilla
    madanale yanaittuyirkku marivaduve
    yidayamena varaiya lagun
    chidaiyanir kunkarpor cadavudali
    navayavattor siruku ranral.

Veru

24. adalina larivumaya mancuddha
    vidayatte yahattaic cerkkun
    caddanaiyal vadanaiga loduvayu
    vodukkamume sarun tane.

Venba

25. akila vupadhi yakanra varive
    dahamac civamen ranisa — mahatte
    yagalad dhiyana madana lahatti
    nakilava satti yagarru.

Viruttam

26. vidhavidhama nilaigalelam vicharan ceydu
    micchaiyaru paramapadam yadon rundo
    vadanaiye didamaga vahattar parri
    yanavarata mulagilvilai yadu vira
    vedusakala vidhamana torran gatku
    metarthamada yahattulado vadaiya rinda
    yadanalap parvaiyinai yagala denru
    masaipo lulagilvilai yadu vira.

27. polimana veluccimagil vurro nagip
    polimanap padaippuverup purro nagip
    polimuyal vantodakka murro nagip
    puraiyilana yulakilvilai yadu vira
    malenumpal kattuvidu patto nagi
    mannusama nagiyella nilaimaik kannum
    velaigalve dattiyaiva veliyir ceydu
    vendiyava rulakilvilai yadu vira.

Venba

28. arivunmai nittana manmavit tava
    narivar pulancerra narta — narivangi
    yavanari vankulisat tankala kalanavan
    savinaimay viranenac charru.

29. tattuvan kandavarkut tame valarumoli
    buddhivalu vumvasantam pondadume — yittaraiyir
    raruvala kadi sakala gunangalun
    cera vilangalenat ter.

30. ceymaiyulan cenrukathai ketparpol vadanaika
    deymanancey dunceyya deyavaika — doymanancey
    dinrenun ceydade yingasaivar runkanavir
    kunreri vilvar kuli.

31. vandituyil vanukkav vandisela nirralodu
    vanditani yurridutan manume — vandiya
    munavuda lulle yurangumeyn nanikku
    manatoli nittaiyurak kam.

32. nanavu kanavutuyi naduvark kappa
    nanavu tuyirruriya namat — tenumat
    turiya madeyuladar ronrumun rinrar
    ruriya vatitan tuni.

33. sanchitava gamiyangal sarava nanikkul
    vinjumenal verrar kelvikkuvilam — buncollam
    bharttapoyk kaimmaiyurap pattiniyen cadadupor
    karttapo muvinaiyun kan.

34. makkan manaivimudan marravarka larpamati
    makkat korukudumba manave — mikkakalvi
    yullavarta mullatte yonralapan nurkudumba
    mulladuyo gattataiya yor.

35. eluttarinda tampiranda dengeyen renni
    yeluttait tolaikka venado — reluttarinden
    sattango lendirattin salburrar sonagiri
    vittagane verar vilambu.

36. karru madangarir kallada reyuyndar
    parru madappeyin palyndar — surrupala
    chintaivay noyuyndar sirtedi yodaluynda
    ruyndadon ranren runai.

37. ella vulagun turumba yinumaraiga
    lellame kaikku lirundalum — pollap
    pugalcciyam vesivasam pukka radimai
    yagalavida lamma varidu.

38. tananri yarundu tannaiya rensolinen
    ranrannai valttuginun talttuginun — tanenna
    tanpiraren roramar rannilaiyir peramar
    ranenru ninridave tan.

39. adduvita menru mahatturuga vorpodu
    madduvitan ceygaiyi larrarka — puttirane
    yadduvita muvulagat tagun guruvino
    dadduvita maga dari.

40. akilave dantasid dhantasa rattai
    yahamunmai yaga varaiva — nahancet
    tahamadu vagi larivuru vamav
    vehamade micca mari.

NOTE ON TRANSLITERATION

Sanskrit

The verses quoted in this book follow the current usage of transliteration of Sanskrit words.

The approximate sound-equivalents of the letters are as follows:

a	-	as *u*	in *hut*
ā	-	as *a*	in *psalm*
i	-	as *i*	in *knit*
ī	-	as *e e*	in *meet*
u	-	as *u*	in *full*
ū	-	as *u*	in *rule*
ṛ	-	as *r*	in fiery (between *ri* and *ru*)
e	-	as *e*	in *they* (always long in Sanskrit)
o	-	as *o*	in *note* (always long in Sanskrit)
ai	-	as *ai*	in *aisle*
au	-	as *o w*	in *fowl*
ṁ	-	anusvara (nasal sound accompanying a vowel)
	-	as *m*	in *sum*
ḥ	-	visarga (sound like light breathing); pronunciation varies according to preceding vowel
'		- apostrophe stands for elided *a*	
k	-	as *k*	in *kite*
kh	-	as *k h*	in *inkhorn*
g	-	as *g*	in *gate*
gh	-	as *g h*	in *springhead*
n	-	as *ng*	in *sing*
c	-	as *ch*	in *church*
ch	-	as *ch h*	in *church-history*
j	-	as *j*	in *jelly*
jh	-	as *ge h*	in *bridge house*
n	-	as *n*	in *new*
t	-	as *t*	in *task*
ṭh	-	as *th*	in *anthill*
ḍ	-	as *d*	in *dark*

ḍh	-	as *dh*	in *Godhead*
ṇ	-	as *n*	in *Monday* (labial articulation)
ṭ	-	as *th*	in *panther*
ṭh	-	as *th*	in *thought*
d	-	as *th*	in *they*
dh	-	as *d h*	in *adhere* (but more dental)
n	-	as *n*	in *note*
p	-	as *p*	in *pan*
ph	-	as *p h*	in *topheavy*
b	-	as *b*	in *bed*
bh	-	as *b h*	in *clubhouse*
m	-	as *m*	in *mill*
y	-	as *y*	in *yet*
r	-	as *r*	in *race*
l	-	as *l*	in *lake*
v	-	as *v*	in *live*
ś	-	as (palatal sibilant) as s in sure	
ṣ	-	as (palatal sibilant) as sh in bush	
s	-	as *s*	in *save*
h	-	as *h*	in *hall*
ḷ	-	as *l*	in *curl*
kṣ	-	as *ks h*	in *baksheesh*

Tamil

Transliteration of Tamil words follows the usual pronunciation and not the written form, *e.g.*, the word that is written as *atu* is pronounced *adu*.

There are no aspirated consonants in Tamil. Where a Tamil word is a derivative from the Sanskrit having an aspirate, the transliteration of the word follows the Sanskrit e.g., *siddhigal*.

In the transliteration, no difference has been made between the two Tamil n's (ந and ன)

The following are the additional letters in Tamil:

r (ற) — hard as in *ring*.

l (ழ) — like *g* in French.

GLOSSARY

Abhava: non-existence, non-being; one of the seven categories of the Vaisheshika philosophy.

Abhinna-nimitta-upadana-karana: the material cause which is non-distinct from the efficient cause. According to Advaita, God is the efficient as well as the material cause of the world.

Abhyasa: repetition; repeated practice; persistent discipline.

Achara: stationary.

Achit: unintelligent; inert; this is a feature of the non-Self.

Adhikarika-muktas: those *jivanmuktas* who, after gaining release, are engaged in the mission of saving the world. Also called *chira-jivins*.

Adrishta: literally 'unseen'; it is the 'unseen potency' generated by good works, which brings about the appropriate result such as enjoyment in heaven in proper time.

Agami-karma: lit. the *karma* that is to come; the results of such deeds as the soul goes on accumulating, and which are to be experienced in a future birth.

Ahankara: egoity.

Ajiva: non-soul; one of the two categories in Jainism, the other being *jiva* (soul).

Ajnani: the ignorant; the one who has not realized the Self.

Akritsna: incomplete, non-whole; whatever is not the Self is an appearance, a part, non-whole, incomplete.

Amanibhava (also *Amanasta*): the state of non-mind, of egolessness.

Amsa: part, aspect, limb.

Amsi: that which has parts, *viz.*, the whole.

Ananda: bliss; one of the terms indicative of the nature of Brahman-Atman.

Anandamayakosha: sheath of bliss; the innermost of the five sheaths covering the soul; it is identified with nescience.

Anava: egoism; lit. that which makes the soul atomic (limited) as it were. In Saiva-Siddhanta, this is the primary defect (*mala*) of the soul.

Anirvachaniya: indeterminable; the world of *maya* is said to be indeterminable, since it is neither real nor unreal.

Annamaya: made of food, *i.e.*, material component; this is the outermost sheath covering the soul; the physical body, also called *sthula-sarira*.

Antahkarana: internal organ or mind; it is internal in contrast to the external sense-organs such as the eyes and the feet.

Apana: one of the five vital airs; its movement is downward.

Apara-vidya: lower or inferior knowledge; this is empirical knowledge, knowledge of phenomena. Even the Vedas are included in this category. Only Brahman-knowledge is the higher knowledge (*para vidya*).

Arthavada: eulogistic or condemnatory statement; this should be interpreted not literally, but only figuratively.

Asana: posture of sitting, steady and comfortable, suitable for meditation.

Asraya: locus, basis, ground, support.

Asti: existence; is one of the three terms employed to indicate the nature of Self, the ultimate reality; the other terms are *bhati* and *priyam*.

Atmalabha: lit. gaining the Self; Self-realization which is not a new acquisition, but which is the realisation of the eternal Self.

Atmanivedana: self-surrender; the offering of the ego to the Lord, or its dissolution in the plenary experience.

Atma-vichara: Self-enquiry; the enquiry into the nature of the Self.

Avarana: obscuration; one of the two functions of *avidya*, the other being *vikshepa* or projection of the illusory world.

Avidya: nescience; according to some Advaitins, it is the individual counterpart of the cosmic *maya*; according to others, there is no difference between *avidya* and *maya*.

Avyakta: unmanifest; it is the state of *prakriti*, where the evolutionary process has not yet commenced.

Bhati: manifestation, which is characteristic of the Self.

Bhaya: fear.

Bheda: difference.

Bhushana: ornament, excellence.

Buddha: the awake; the perfect one; one who has gained release from bondage.

Buddhi: understanding, intellect.

Chara: moving.

Chatushkoti: the four-pronged dialectic, involving the altenatives (a) is, (b) is not, (c) both, and (d) neither.

Chidabhasa: reflection of Intelligence (Self) in the internal organ; this is the individual soul (*jiva*), the pseudo-'I'.

Chirajivin: the long-lived; the *adhikarikamukta* is called by this name.

Chit: intelligence; one of the terms indicative of the nature of Brahman-Atman.

Chitta: mind.

Darshan: lit. sight or seeing; a philosophical perspective, a school of philosophy.

Dharma: religious duty; righteousness, good deed; merit (also called *punya*).

Dhira: one who is steady, firm, brave; a hero.

Dhyana: meditation, contemplation.

Dravya: substance.

Dushana: defect.

Guna: constituent of *prakriti*, in the Sankhya system, quality; what is secondary.

Heyaguna: despicable quality; trait that should be abandoned.

Hiranyagarbha: lit. the golden embryo; name of the Lord in the form of the subtle universe.

Hridayagranthi: lit. the knot of the heart; the coupling of the true and the untrue, the Self and the not-Self, which is due to ignorance.

Iccha: desire.

Isvara: God, the supreme Being as the world-ground; the supreme object of worship, endowed with all auspicious qualities.

Jagat: the world-process.

Jiva: the individual soul.

Jivanmukta: one who is released while living in the body.

Jivanmukti: release while living in the body.

Jnana: knowledge, cognition.

Jnanendriya: organ of knowledge; there are five such organs: those of hearing, touch, sight, taste and smell.

Jnani: lit. the one who knows; the wise one who knows the Self.

Jnata: knower, cognizer.

Jneya: object of knowledge, cognized object.

Jyotishtoma: a sacrifice of an optional kind, to be performed by one who desires heaven; this is a Soma sacrifice.

Kamakala: lit. The aspect of desire. In the Tantrika system, it means the splendour of the Lord, consisting of the three *gunas* of *prakriti* or *maya*.

Kamyakarma: deed for a desired end; optional rite which is performed for gaining certain ends like prosperity in this world and enjoyment in heaven.

Karanasarira: the causal body; nescience which is the primal cause of *samsara*.

Karma: action; fruit of action; in the Vaisheshika system, *karma* means motion.

Karmendriya: organs of action or motor organs, *viz.*, of speech, grasping, locomotion, excretion and generation.

Kosha: sheath; there are said to be five sheaths covering or limiting the soul.

Kriya: act; will.

Kritakritya: one who has accomplished all that has to be accomplished; the perfect one.

Laukika: secular; what belongs to this world.

Lokasamgraha: welfare of the world; commonwealth.

Mahasamadhi: lit. the great quiescence; the passing away of a sage is usually referred to by this term; also the tomb that enshrines the remains of such a one.

Mahat: lit. the great; the first evolute of *prakriti* in the Sankhya system: also called *buddhi*.

Manomaya: lit. made of mind; one of the five sheaths enveloping the soul.

Mauna: silence, the state of quiescence.

Maya: cosmic ignorance which is responsible for world-appearance.

Moksha: release.

Mokshakama; desire for release.

Mukta: the released one.

Naimittikakarma: occasional rites to be performed on specific occasions, such as the birth of a son.

Nama: name; one of the three categories constituting the world. The others are: *rupa* and *karma*; *nama* stands for all mental phenomena and *rupa* for all physical phenomena.

Nityakarma: obligatory rites; those rites which are to be performed without dependence on inclination.

Nityanityavastuviveka: discrimination of the eternal from the non-eternal. This is one of the qualifications a prospective student of Vedanta should possess,

Paramartha: supreme truth; ultimate or absolute reality.

Paravidya: higher or superior knowledge, *i.e.*, knowledge of the ultimate reality, Brahman-Atman.

Pasa: bonds that bind the soul; according to Saivism, there are three bonds, *anava*, *karma* and *maya*.

Pasu: lit. cattle, any tethered animal. The soul is referred to as *pasu*, esp. in Saivism, as it is dependent on God, and as it is in the condition of bondage in *samsara*.

Pati: the Lord; this is the designation of God (Siva), especially in Saivism.

Prabodha: awakening, illumination, enlightenment.

Prakasa: illumination, effulgence; same as *chit*.

Prakriti: primal nature; prius of evolution, in Sankhya system.

Pramana: means of valid knowledge.

Pramata: knower, cognizer.

Prameya: object of valid knowledge.

Pramiti: knowledge resulting from the operation of a means of valid knowledge.

Prana: one of the five vital airs, which goes forward; also the general name for the five vital airs.

Pranamaya: lit. made of *prana*; one of the five sheaths, consisting of vital air.

Pranayama: regulation and control of breath; one of the steps in *Yoga*.

Prapancha: the world, so called because it has five characteristics: existence, manifestation, lovability, name and form.

Prarabdhakarma: *karma* that has begun to fructify; the portion of the *karma* of previous lives that is responsible for the present life.

Pratipakshabhavana : contemplating the contrary; this is a technique in *Yoga* by which one gets rid of false notions.

Pratisiddhakarma: prohibited actions; deeds that are forbidden in the Veda.

Priyam: lovability; one of the terms that indicates the nature of the Self.

Punya: merit, the result of good deeds.

Purna: full, plenum; one of the terms which indicates the nature of the Self.

Purusha: spirit, self; in Sankhya system, *purusha* and *prakriti* are the two primary categories.

Purushakara: human effort.

Rajas: activity; one of the three constituents of *prakriti*, in the Sankhya system.

Rupa: form; see *nama*.

Sadhaka: lit. one who adopts a means; spiritual aspirant.

Sadhana: discipline, means.

Sahaja: lit. natural; one's natural state as the pure Self.

Sahaja-sthiti: one's natural state; see *Sahaja*.

Sakshichaitanya: witness-consciousness; the Self as the witness of all experience.

Samanya: generality; one of the seven categories of the Vaisheshikas.

Samavaya: inherence; intimate relation as between a substance and its qualities, between a whole and its parts, etc. This is a category in the Nyaya-Vaisheshika system.

Samadhi: abstract meditation, intense concentration; the final stage in *Yoga*.

Samana: one of the five vital airs that equalizes what is eaten and drunk.

Samsara: transmigration.

Sanchita: lit. what has been accumulated; accumulated deeds of past lives which are yet to bear fruit.

Sandhyavandana: prayer that is offered to the Lord in the morning and in the evening when day and night meet.

Sannyasin: one who has renounced the world; *sannyasa* is the fourth stage in life.

Saptabhanginaya: The sevenfold mode of predication; according to Jainism the seven modes are: (1) is, (2) is not, (3) is and is not, (4) is inexpressible, (5) is and is inexpressible, (6) is not and is inexpressible and (7) is, is not and is inexpressible.

Sat: existence, being, reality.

Sattva: purity, goodness; one of the three constituents of *prakriti*.

Sruti: lit. what is heard; scripture, revelation.

Sthitaprajna: one whose wisdom has become steady; the perfect one.

Sthulasarira: the gross-body; the physical body; same as *annamaya kosha*.

Suddhachinmatram: pure consciousness; the pure Self.

Sukshmasarira: the subtle body, consisting of *prana*, sense-organs, and mind.

Sunya: void; may be interpreted to mean either absolute void or void as it were; the latter sense would not distinguish *sunya* from Brahman-Atman.

Sunyavada: the doctrine of the Madhyamika Buddhist that void is the reality.

Svasthya: sound state, health; one's real nature.

Tamas: darkness; one of the three constituents of *prakriti* in the Sankhya system. It means also ignorance.

Tapas: lit. warmth, heat; austerity, penance, meditation.

Trigunatmakavibhuti: splendour of the ultimate reality consisting of the three *gunas: sattva, rajas* and *tamas*. Same as *Kama-kala.*

Triputi: the triple factors in knowledge situation, *viz.*, cognizer, cognized object and cognitive process.

Trivritkarana: process of triplication by which three primary elements combine to produce the world.

Turiya: lit. the fourth; the transcendent reality which is Brahman-Atman; it is called the fourth because it transcends the three states of experience, waking, dream and sleep. It is not the fourth in *addition* to those three; it is their basic reality.

Turiyatita: lit, beyond *turiya*; but in fact it is the same as *turiya*: it is the transcendent reality which is at the same time the basis of all experience.

Turiya-turiya: same as *turiyatita*.

Udana: the upgoing vital air. See *apana*.

Vaidika: pertaining to the Veda.

Vajra: lit. the hard and mighty one; a thunderbolt; weapon of Indra, said to have been formed out of the bones of the sage Dadici.

Vasanas: latent impressions left on the mind by past experiences.

Videhamukti: release gained after the death of the body.

Vijnamaya: lit. made of intellect, one of the sheaths that envelop the soul.

Vikshepa: projection; the power of *avidya* whereby the illusory world is projected.

Vimarsa: lit. reflection, consideration; in *Sakta-tantra*, the power by which the world is created.

Virat: lit. ruler, sovereign; name of the Lord in the form of the gross universe.

Vishaya: object, content.

Visesha: particularity; speciality.

Vyana: one of the five vital airs that goes in all directions.

Vyavahara: empirical usage; temporal experience.

INDEX

R

Ramakrishna, Sri 65, 95, 97
Ramanuja 38
Realism 50, 95

S

Saiva Siddhanta 31, 170
Samadhi 8, 10, 128, 176
Sankara, 12, 18, 22-24, 28, 31, 45, 52, 70, 79, 103, 115, 138, 140-144
Sat 20-22, 25, 33, 44, 94, 102, 141, 176
Sankhya 35, 36, 38, 39, 48, 67, 95, 130, 172, 175, 177
Scepticism 25
Self-enquiry (atma-vichara) 19, 49, 92, 96, 97, 100, 107, 109, 112, 115, 118-120, 125, 138-140, 144, 148, 171,
Sunyavada 75, 177
Sutra-bhashya 44, 138, 140

T

Tiruvannamalai 1, 3, 5-13, 15, 16, 135, 143, 147, 148
Turiya 96, 128, 177,

U

Ulladu Narpadu 21-23, 50, 151
Upadesasaram 18
Upanishad 47, 48, 51, 52, 65, 68, 70, 71, 117, 137, 139, 146
    Brihadaranyaka 34, 44, 50-53, 57, 61, 65, 87, 106
    Chandogya 22,33, 48, 76, 102, 139
    Katha 27, 29, 58, 62, 68, 91, 137
    Kena 89, 91
    Mandukya 23, 59, 60
    Mundaka 34
    Svetasvatara 30, 34
    Taittiriya 54, 70, 82